REINVENTION

Ours is the era of "reinvention". From psychotherapy to life coaching, from self-help manuals to cosmetic surgery, and from corporate rebranding to urban redesign: the art of reinvention is inextricably interwoven with the lure of the next frontier, the breakthrough to the next boundary – especially boundaries of the self.

In this insightful and provocative book, Anthony Elliott examines "reinvention" as a key buzzword of our times. Through a wide-ranging and impassioned assessment, Elliott reviews the new global forms of reinvention – from reinvention gurus to business reinvention, from personal makeovers to corporate rebrandings. In doing so, he undertakes a serious if often amusing consideration of contemporary reinvention practices, including super-fast weight loss diets, celebrity makeovers, body augmentations, speed dating, online relationship therapies, organizational restructurings, business downsizings and many more.

This absorbing book is an ideal introduction to the topic of reinvention for students and general readers alike. *Reinvention* offers a provocative and radical reflection on an issue (sometimes treated as trivial in the public sphere) that is increasingly politically urgent in terms of its personal, social and environmental consequences.

Anthony Elliott is Director of the Hawke Research Institute, where he is Research Professor of Sociology at the University of South Australia.

SHORTCUTS – *"Little Books on Big Issues"*

Shortcuts is a major new series of concise, accessible introductions to some of the major issues of our times. The series is developed as an A to Z coverage of emergent or new social, cultural and political phenomena. Issues and topics covered range from food to fat, from climate change to suicide bombing, from love to zombies. Whilst the principal focus of **Shortcuts** is the relevance of current issues, topics and debates to the social sciences and humanities, the books should also appeal to a wider audience seeking guidance on how to engage with today's leading social, political and philosophical debates.

Series Editor: Anthony Elliott is a social theorist, writer and Director of the Hawke Research Institute, where he is Research Professor of Sociology at the University of South Australia. He is also Visiting Research Professor in the Department of Sociology at the Open University, UK, and Visiting Professor in the Department of Sociology at University College Dublin, Ireland. His writings have been published in sixteen languages, and he has written widely on, amongst other topics, identity, globalization, society, celebrity and mobilities.

Titles in the series:

**For Zygmunt Bauman
and Bo-Magnus Salenius**

REINVENTION

Anthony Elliott

Routledge
Taylor & Francis Group

LONDON AND NEW YORK

First published 2013
by Routledge
2 Park Square, Milton Park, Abingdon, Oxon OX14 4RN

Simultaneously published in the USA and Canada
by Routledge
711 Third Avenue, New York, NY 10017

*Routledge is an imprint of the Taylor & Francis Group,
an informa business*

British Library Cataloguing in Publication Data
A catalogue record for this book is available from the
British Library

Library of Congress Cataloging-in-Publication Data
Elliott, Anthony, 1964–
Reinvention / Anthony Elliott.
   p. cm. – (Shortcuts)
Includes bibliographical references and index.
1. Change. 2. Civilization, Modern–21st century. I. Title.
CB430.E45 2013
303.4–dc23   2012021962

ISBN: 978-0-415-68283-1 (hbk)
ISBN: 978-0-415-68284-8 (pbk)
ISBN: 978-0-203-07970-6 (ebk)

Typeset in Bembo
by Taylor & Francis Books

MIX
Paper from
responsible sources
FSC
www.fsc.org   FSC® C004839

Printed and bound in Great Britain by
TJ International Ltd, Padstow, Cornwall

CONTENTS

FOREWORD

Shortcuts is a major new series of concise, accessible introductions to some of the major issues of our times. The series is developed as an A to Z coverage of emergent or new social, cultural and political phenomena. Issues and topics covered range from food to fat, from climate change to suicide bombing, from love to zombies. Whilst the principal focus of *Shortcuts* is the relevance of current issues, topics and debates to the social sciences and humanities, the books should also appeal to a wider audience seeking guidance on how to engage with today's leading social, political and philosophical debates.

Self-help manuals, speed dating, cybertherapy, personal makeover, cosmetic surgery, life coaching, super-fast dieting, career redesign and corporate rebranding: welcome to life in a world addicted to reinvention. In this concise, stylish and provocative investigation of the culture of reinvention, acclaimed sociologist Anthony Elliott looks afresh at how contemporary women and men seek to refashion their personal and professional lives and asks what are the key institutional drivers of reinvention. The book is an exhilarating, and sometimes disturbing, tour through the thickets of what Elliott terms our "reinvention society". *Reinvention* is an essential *Shortcut*.

Gerhard Boomgaarden
Senior Publisher

ACKNOWLEDGMENTS

Some of the material in this book was delivered in a different form as the Agnes Heller Lecture at La Trobe University, Melbourne, in 2009, and as the keynote lecture to the Society for Sociological Theory in Japan at Chiba University in 2010. I am deeply thankful to my hosts at these institutions – especially John Carroll, Masataka Katagiri and Atsushi Sawai – for their warm hospitality. I am also greatly indebted, as always, to the professional input and friendship of my editor Gerhard Boomgaarden. Thanks also to Emily Briggs at Routledge. Zygmunt Bauman has and continues to advise me well; I am indebted to him for the many ways in which he has helped me over the years. Charles Lemert read the manuscript – in-flight between Adelaide and Sydney – and made terrific last minute suggestions; he has been a most loyal and generous friend. Nicola Geraghty also contributed substantially to the book, and I am deeply grateful for her assistance and support throughout. David Radford provided terrific administrative and editorial support, and I am indebted to him for numerous suggestions. Finally, special thanks to the establishment where I have been privileged to have space to think widely and creatively on the topic of reinvention – namely, LearningMiles in Finland. In this connection, the contributions of Bo-Magnus Salenius, Ralf Blomqvist, Ingrid Biese and Camilla Sigfrids have been paramount.

Anthony Elliott
Adelaide, 2012

ACKNOWLEDGMENTS

INTRODUCTION

The rise of reinvention

In 2012, *The New York Times* published an article titled "Bridal Hunger Games". The article analysed the trials and tribulations of women seeking to lose weight in time for their wedding day. Various experts on bridal weight loss training contributed reflections on the most effective ways for women to downsize, detox and thereby reinvent their bodies. Typical weight loss for contemporary "training brides", so the article reported, is 15 to 20 pounds. The contemporary bridal training menu is one focused resolutely on reinvention; from detoxing cleanses to fat-busting diets, training brides are out to demonstrate to others a complete *transformation* of their bodies. Downsizing yourself for the big day involves a curious kind of devotion to the task at hand, one in which denial and deprivation are central to the mantras of reinvention. Yet in current times it helps, in reinventing your body, to be assured that the desired transformation can be achieved the speediest way possible. It is for this reason alone that drastic diets – designed to deliver super-fast weight loss – have become all the rage in the current regime of bridal hunger games.

Even so, drastic reinvention can always be pushed further. Transgression is, as it were, built in to the very logic of makeover culture and reinvention society. One latest fad amongst drastic diets involves daily injections of a hormone associated with pregnancy – human chorionic gonadotropin. Notwithstanding various health warnings from government agencies, clinics across the United States have offered the hormone – along with guidelines in self-administering the injections – to those seeking the latest in body downsizing. This may, at first glance, sound like a kind of living death, but according to *The New York Times* it is a procedure which has become increasingly popular with many training brides.

Another fad for contemporary reinvention consumers is Diet Tube, a procedure for reinvention pioneered in Italy. Consumers of Diet Tube are provided with liquid nutrients which pass through a piece of plastic tubing, which is inserted directly into the nose. Attached to the tubing is a micro-electric pump, which injects protein-filled liquid directly into the stomach to keep hunger at bay. One might be forgiven for thinking that a nasogastric tube inserted up a nostril is the last thing that citizens of the contemporary West might imagine desiring, or doing. On the contrary, however, Diet Tube has become increasingly popular – not only amongst training brides, but more generally for women (and some men) seeking out extreme reinvention. Indeed, this drastic diet of reinvention has been viewed by media critics as a kind of fashion statement, akin to carrying a Prada bag or wearing Gucci sunglasses. As the Next New Diet, such reinvention is represented as at once an indispensible bridge to personal change and a transformed body on the one hand, and a means for disciplining and regulating the individual self on the other.

In contrast to cosmetic surgical procedures designed to suck out and re-sculpt fat, and which always require both "down time" and a recovery period on the part of the patient, Diet Tube requires of its users only that they do not eat (apart from, perhaps, the consuming of green tea). This, in itself, indicates that we are dealing with a desire for reinvention held in thrall to the logics of excess, or of what Freud termed the "death drive". In the name of a desire for total reinvention, the body is wrenched from nature and the self is rendered omnipotent.

For it is precisely in this mixing of not eating on the one hand, and having a tube supply protein-filled liquid to the stomach on the other, that Diet Tube stands out as a fashionable new departure – as the Next New Diet – for consumers of reinvention society. Consider journalist Amanda Mitchison's reflections on a young woman she interviewed who was experimenting with Diet Tube:

> The tube, she says, didn't restrict her lifestyle. When she went out, she just popped the pump into her Prada bag and nobody in the street seemed to notice she had a tube up her nose. I find this surprising. Normally you notice when people have tubes up their noses, just as you also notice when they are wearing gas masks. But Rome is Rome.

> *(Mitchison 2012)*

What Mitchison finds surprising – that fellow consumers do not notice a piece of tubing inserted into the nose – is, in fact, an essential aspect of the denial practised today throughout reinvention societies. Consumers, such as the young women trialling Diet Tube, might tell themselves and say to others that such activities are not noticed, or that they wish such activities to go undetected. But this is where the boundaries between fantasy and reality blur, because a demonstration to others of the project of self-transformation is built in to the very fabric of reinvention society. Undertaking the latest reinvention product or service on the market confers a pleasurable sense of status and superiority. And this is one reason for the rapid rise of Diet Tube, which has recently opened centres not only in Italy but also in Barcelona, Madrid and Athens.

If obesity today is an epidemic of global consequence – the World Health Organization recognized that obesity was a global epidemic as long ago as 1997 – our preoccupation with dieting and super-fast weight loss is equally sweeping in its global reach.

One of the most interesting things about the global diet industry is that it trades on people's craving for the Next New Diet. The constant barrage of diet-related research captured and conveyed by 24/7 mass media is one powerful indicator of contemporary women and men's wishful fantasies for slimmer, sexier bodies; the rise of the multi-billion dollar slimming industry is also suggestive of the ubiquity of the desire for reinvention throughout modern societies. The spawning of extreme reinvention practices designed to shed the pounds of Western consumers, many of whom have been rendered hair-raisingly fat (and fatter) by the global fast food industry, reflects a festering culture of instant change and fast solutions. Shot through with the illusions of celebrity culture, the inherent plasticity of reinvention is perhaps nowhere better dramatized than in the relentless diversification and displacement of fashionable diets. From the Atkins Diet to the Dukan Diet, the Zone Diet to the Scarsdale Diet, the onion diet to the cabbage diet: the austerely self-disciplined regimens of fat-busting are revealed as part of the feverish work of reinvention, in which tracking and trialling the latest fad diet appears as an essential precondition to human flourishing. The professional terrain of super-fast dieting – of private nutritionists, personal trainers, calorie counsellors and diet trainers – has in recent years given way to ever more drastic, excessive reinvention practices in the search for innovative ways to reduce fat. Diet Tube is just one of the latest "innovations" to be made available in the reinvention marketplace. Like other drastic diets, the aim is to make a reinvention statement out of fat busting.

Reinvention society

Ours is the era of "reinvention". Today's "cultures of reinvention" seem for many definitive of the perfect lifestyle. From super-fast dieting to life coaching, from reality television to cosmetic surgery: the art of reinvention is inextricably interwoven with the lure of the next frontier, the break through to the next boundary, especially boundaries of the self. For others, however, the twenty-first century craze for reinvention represents the degradation of culture, the narcissistic illusions of a me-generation, and thus only fit for satirical mauling by the likes of, say, Tina Fey or Germaine Greer.

In this book, I want to set the idea of reinvention in what I hope is a more original context, one which is sociological in analysis but which also pays close attention to the emotional impacts and consequences of our fascination with makeover culture and the global spread of reinvention. In developing the argument that reinvention has become a central driver of both personal and global life, or private and institutional fields, I review an extensive range of social practices currently transforming twenty-first century societies. The book ranges from reinvention gurus to business reinvention, from personal makeovers to corporate rebranding. In doing so, I undertake a serious, if often amusing consideration of contemporary reinvention practices including super-fast weight loss diets, celebrity makeovers, body augmentations, speed dating, online relationship therapies, organizational restructurings, business downsizings and many more. Throughout, my hope is that *Reinvention* offers a provocative and radical reflection on an issue (sometimes treated as trivial in the public sphere) that is increasingly politically urgent in terms of its personal, social and environmental consequences.

The ultimate global makeover

If reinvention reigns supreme, it is because flexibility, adaptability and transformation have become intricately interwoven with the global electronic economy. In a world of endless corporate lay-offs, institutional off-shorings and company reorganizations, people are scrambling to adjust to new definitions and experiences of self, relationships, intimacies, work and many others. Against the backdrop of this brave new world of globalization, the communications revolution and computer-based production technology, it is hardly surprising that contemporary women and men express a wish – registered in ever-increasing numbers – to instantly transform their lives, to self-fashion without restraint or resistance. Like contestants from the reality television programme *Extreme Makeover* – where people undergo cosmetic surgery, dental work, exercise regimens and wardrobe redesign in order to refashion their lives – more and more men and women believe people can and should recreate their lives in whatever ways they choose. In this narcissistic condition, the self is recast as a do-it-yourself assembly kit. Reality becomes magically deflated, as there are no longer any constraints imposed by society, at the same time that the self is inflated to the level of a work of art.

Behind this endless proliferation of the reinvention spectacle there lies a cultural imperative to act – to fix, remake, enhance or transform. Reinvent now! Join in. If you do not enjoy your current lifestyle or do not like how you presently look, discard and redesign. In this sense, the cultural imperative to reinvention involves a thorough going self-fashioning, one that arguably involves an augmentation and not diminishing of the individual self. Even so, however, the creative dimensions of identity rein-vented would appear troublingly close to a nihilistic liquidation of it. Contemporary women and men are instructed on the one hand that their lives can be reinvented however they fancy; but for the same reason an endless refashioning of self soon enough leads to an obliteration of value or meaning on the other hand. It is as if, drunk on the narcissistic fantasies of the ego, the endlessly self-fashioning individual of reinvention society is revealed as a compulsive neurotic, addicted to repeating the highs and lows of a life made over, again and again.

To be sure, society in the twenty-first century propagates a master idea: it is through reinvention that we affirm ourselves and legitimate our experiences. When people in modern society come to think about the conditions and consequences of their lives – of current dilemmas as well as future risks, to say nothing of remembered pasts – reinvention seems desirable. In this connection, the lure of reinvention is that it is inextricably interwoven with the dream of "something else". It does so in various ways, and one of the aims of this book is to critique – in a provisional and necessarily restricted manner – the interconnected processes underpinning the explosive compound of societies of reinvention. But let us begin simply by sketching some of the ways – some straightforward, others more subtle – in which reinvention reshapes the lives of people and the organizations and institutions of which they are part. I will begin by offering some "snapshots" of current practices of reinvention (picked somewhat randomly), shifting from the realm of the individual self to the sphere of work and family life to the collective level of groups and organizations.

If fashion, fitness and food are all central examples of lifestyle reinvention in contemporary culture, the prime example of it is surely cosmetic surgery. From Botox and liposuction to tummy tucks and mini-facelifts, this remorseless technology of reinvention casts down from the dizzying heights of celebrity culture, fills the screens of reality television, and looms large in the lives of many millions seeking to find a way to make the burdens of daily life more bearable. Cosmetic surgery, in other words, is arguably the most graphic representation of the reinvention idiom we are tracing – and I shall look at the rise of cosmetic surgical culture and the makeover industries in some detail in Chapter 1. Yet cosmetic surgery as a technology of reinvention extends well beyond the realm of appearances as conventionally understood, offering as it does a manufactured transformation of the human body itself.

Consider, for example, the recent worldwide spread of demand for cosmetic gynaecology. From North America to Europe to Asia, aesthetic vaginal surgery has become one of the fastest growing cosmetic procedures in a global makeover business worth billions of dollars. Procedures increasingly undertaken – largely by women of the polished, expensive cities of the West – include labiaplasty (trimming or removal of the labia), hymenoplasty (or "revirgi-nation"), and vaginal rejuvenation (a procedure for tightening). The motivation of women seeking what the industry terms "designer vaginas" has been the topic of hot debate in recent media analysis. From rising health concerns about discomfort during sex to the global spread of raunch culture, the vagina has been cast as a new body-part for commercial reinvention – or as the authors of a study in the *British Journal of Obstetrics and Gynaecology* put it, "a viable site for beautification and normal-ization" (in Freeman-Greene 2009). Like Britney Spears' pelvic dance thrusts, cosmetic surgeons believe in the infinite plasticity of women's genitalia. This fretting over genitalia, like Brazilian waxes and suburban pole dancing, is infused by the notion that it is a supreme achievement of the individual to remake her body – in the frame of a pre-pubescent beauty ideal – as an object of sensuous decadence. Yet there may also be a more bland narcissism at work here too. Australian-based plastic surgeon, Dr Kourosh Tavakoli, embodies this contradiction by speaking of aesthetic vaginal surgery as heralding "a mental transformation" (in Freeman-Greene 2009), whilst simulta-neously declaring that women who have undergone such pro-cedures can wear a leotard or bikini with newfound confidence. Clearly, the psychological costs of reinvention can be stunningly high – and perhaps especially for women. But as journalist Suzy Freeman-Greene contends:

> It seems astounding that women would endure such pain and cost merely to look subtly different in a leotard. Far more plausible is a link between the widespread availability of porn, the popularity of Brazilians and the growth of labioplasty. Left to their natural hirsute state, how many people would even notice the shape of their genitals?
>
> *(Freeman-Greene 2009)*

The reinvention craze is not only, as the critics sometimes claim, limited to the private sphere, to personality and lifestyle change, to image and the body; it is rather a dynamic, inter-personal, constantly transforming process. Thus it is the case that reinvention has loomed large in the working out of new methods and ventures which contemporary women and men have fashioned in the renegotiation of professional and personal life. Consider the Life Maximizer study from Microsoft, which reported in 2009 that over three-quarters of working profes-sionals in modern societies are "life-splicing" – defined as a mixing up of social life with work. The general idea is that people are "life-splicing" when they are, for example, shopping online or exploring dating websites whilst at work in the office; the flipside also holds true, with the splicing of life evidenced by the increasing number of professionals answering work emails whilst reclining on the couch at home in front of the television. A senior manager from Microsoft's research division, Ashley Highfield, explains this reinvention of work/life balance thus: "It seems the idea of life versus work is well and truly dead – it's no longer that clear cut, as thanks to technology we are multi-tasking and life-splicing minute by minute" (see Microsoft's "Life Maximizer Study" online).

There are, to be sure, collective kinds of reinvention too, those of the group, organization or corporation. The con-temporary fashion for perpetual reinvention is thus at once personal and cultural, emotional and institutional, however much its devotees might imagine it springs from the energies of a monadic self. It is exactly this double-edged coding of reinvention which comes to the fore in various collective reme-dies developed in response to current social and political problems issuing from globalization. Consider, for example, the powerful growth of those people who declare no religious affiliation today. This has been an especially consequential development for various religious denominations, and has been cast as a consequence of the globalization of consumerism, transformations in popular culture, and a breakdown in the moral fabric of modern societies. Yet it is instructive to consider how some religious groups have sought to respond to sharp membership declines.

The answer, in a nutshell: reinvention. In 2011, the *Los Angeles Times* reported on a small, seemingly insignificant, convention, which launched with a martini reception in Las Vegas. Perhaps hardly the most radical convention launch for Sin City, except that this convention was organized by the Rabbinical Assembly, the conservative arm of Judaism in the United States. Organizers of the convention emphasized, against a backdrop of diminishing conservative synagogue membership and associated financial strains, the need to rethink, restructure and indeed rebrand the institutions of Jewish life. How might such a rebranding of Jewish religion occur? As David Roozen, director of the Hartford Institute for Religion Research, argued: "It's one thing for a corporation to say 'We're going to reinvent ourselves'. A religion can evolve, it can be reinterpreted, you can express it in a different style, but you can't just be doing Judaism one day and say 'I'm going to sell cars' the next" (in Landsberg 2011). That said, a kind of reinvention of Conservative Judaism did emerge from the convention. This consisted of plans ranging from an elimination of membership dues for synagogues to the introduction of an à la carte "fee-for-service" programmes. Rebranding was also high on the agenda, in which discussion of the slogan "A Judaism of Relationships" featured prominently.

Outline of the book

This book is not intended as a straightforward academic study of reinvention. Rather, in seeking to popularize the topic and address a wider public audience, the focus of the book is reflective, analytical and satirical. The genealogy I trace for reinvention, all the way from the reinvention of bodies and persons to reinvented global corporations and networks, may look academically unsystematic. Whilst I try to identify some structuring institutional features of reinvention society throughout the discussion that follows, I should note that the social theory that informs my analysis is worn, as they say, rather loosely on the sleeve. My general argument is that reinvention and its related ideologies are best grasped as a consequence of the spread of a "new individualism" sweeping the expensive, polished cities of the West and beyond. The reinvention craze unleashed by new individualism is structured by four major institutional drivers: self-reinvention; instant change; speed or social acceleration; and short-termism. But I do not discuss in any sociological detail the conditions and consequences of these institutional drivers, as my focus is instead the terrain of reinvention itself. Readers searching for a more detailed sociological analysis might wish to consult my book with Charles Lemert, *The New Individualism: The Emotional Costs of Globalization* (London and New York: Routledge, 2009, 2nd Edition).

1

THE REINVENTION OF BODIES

Our culture of reinvention is perhaps nowhere more evident than at the level of the body, which consumer society presents as a key site for enhancements, transformations and remouldings. From patented crèmes to diet pills to breast implants, ours is the age of body reshaping, recontouring, upgrading and updating. Reality television programmes, such as *10 Years Younger*, *Extreme Makeover* and *Cosmetic Surgery Live*, advance this cultural pre-occupation with changes to the body. Magazines and tabloid newspapers relentlessly track possible cosmetic and surgical enhancements to celebrity bodies. Billboards worldwide advertise digitally enhanced, photoshopped images of slender, sleek and stylized bodies. To be sure, the body has become the persona-lized space of self-reinvention *par excellence*.

This preoccupation with refashioning and reinvention – the era in which "drastic plastic" reigns supreme – was momentarily brought into stark confrontation with itself in 2011, when news spread across the globe of a mother injecting her eight-year-old daughter with Botox. The mother, a beautician based in the

UK, was reportedly using Botox and other fillers on her daughter's face – injecting her forehead, lips and around the eyes – in order to improve the girl's chances of winning a child beauty pageant. The child, according to the mother's account, would one day become a star as a result of these cosmetic measures. Media reports also noted that the child underwent a "virgin wax monthly", so as to prevent any possible development of pubic hairs prior to the child reaching puberty. Indeed, the mother discussed in interview the possibility of her daughter undertaking in the near future procedures such as eyebrow waxing, as well as top-end surgical procedures including breast implants.

This media story, perhaps hardly surprisingly given the child's age, generated strong disbelief in some, horror in others, and moral outrage in many. Part of the cultural shock over this little girl's regular injections of Botox, arguably, concerned an uncomfortable societal awareness of the pervasiveness of a disturbed relationship with bodies – to such a degree that disaffection now infiltrates attitudes towards children's bodies too. Yet in addition to such awareness, there might also have been some appreciation – and related fear? – of the infinite plasticity of the body. Today, regularly and routinely, advertising and media inform that the human body can now be reinvented however one chooses. Bodies are open to improvement, remoulding, resculpting, enhancement and transformation. There are, literally, no limits to body reinvention. You are the architect of your own body – its shape, contours and appearance – and so it is you, in our culture of intensive new individualism, that will be judged favourably on looking good – or not!

In this chapter, I shall examine some key features of contemporary transformations to bodies in our time of intensive reinvention. The chapter introduces two areas of current bodily transformation and reinvention: the first section examines the cosmetics industry; the second section reviews cosmetic surgical culture and the makeover industries. Throughout I shall consider the rich variety of bodily transformation practices from the standpoint of reinvention society.

The skin game

In 2011, supermodel Kate Moss appeared on billboards and in glossy magazines worldwide advertising cosmetics and perfume for Christian Dior. The marketing campaign was "Dior Addict", in which – with Brigitte Bardot inspired cat-eyes and pouting lips – Moss gazed directly at the camera/viewer, gripping a lipstick designed to cast her as an ever-so-famous addict. In one stroke, Moss managed to combine sex appeal and addiction, mixing glamour with vulnerability in stylized proportion. The "Dior Addict" marketing campaign captures well the extent to which addiction now functions as a kind of "cultural short-hand" for fashionable reinvention. From cosmetic maintenance to diet fads to plastic surgery, we can see an addiction to "body redesign" turned into profit.

Consumer culture, according to the late French sociologist Jean Baudrillard, multiplies and accelerates the compulsive excesses of body reshaping. Baudrillard's notion of a "hyperreal world" – of contemporary women and men obsessed with the hyper-slim, the hyper-fit and the hyper-sexual – is one of addiction incarnate. Consumerism and addiction, on this viewpoint, sit together cheek by jowl. In contemporary societies of reinvention, consumer culture is rendered sublime, charged as it is with reconciling the complex contradictions of desire and disappointment, emotion and emptiness. If there is something intoxicating about consumerism it is not only because it trades in extravagant expectations, but because it deceives as well as seduces. Simultaneously holding out the promise of scintillating style and yet frustrating fulfilment at every turn, consumerism inhabits a terrain of lethal ecstasy – each repeated frustration of desire helping to unleash, in turn, new desires or fresh appetites.

Consumer culture thus seduces, enthrals, overwhelms and, ultimately, traumatizes.

If consumer culture in contemporary society diagnoses the human body as flawed, the cosmetics industry is on hand with purported solutions of repair. Successful cosmetics companies, in offering quick-fix solutions to signs of bodily ageing, build upon a deep cultural anxiety that bodies require ongoing work in order to measure up to contemporary standards of health, beauty and sex appeal. From patented crèmes to celebrity-endorsed lotions, the cosmetics industry brands beauty as a personal project of self-realization and self-reconstruction, as something that with ongoing effort – cash, care and discipline – can be achieved. From this angle, the advertising and promotion of cosmetic products – lipstick, mascara, blusher colours – underscores the various sites of the body that demand ongoing "beauty work". Indeed, sociologist Celia Lury has argued that today we witness a sharp proliferation of areas of the body to which the cosmetics industries offer beauty products and solutions. Lips, eyelashes, finger nails, skin, cheeks, shoulders, elbows, armpits, legs and feet: these and other body-parts, as represented in advertising from the cosmetics and style industries, require continual attention, work, repair and renewal.

Against a global media backdrop of unprecedented visual scrutiny of bodies and commercial imagery of sex, the wide-spread cultural anxiety that body-parts require ongoing, routine and vigilant work or attention is raised to the second power. "Maintaining one's body" has become a central preoccupation of contemporary women and men, and there are two key ways in which the cosmetics industry promotes this urge to self-maintenance, self-enhancement and self-remaking. The first is through reference in advertising and promotions to the "threats" of ageing, and its associated connections with bodily decay. As a result of the intricate connections between beauty, youth and sex appeal, so some cultural analysts have argued, people (and especially women) are put on "high alert" to detect any signs of ageing and related "bodily faults". Here the youth aesthetic – which directly ties age to sexual beauty – is pivotal to the selling of cosmetics.

The second way in which the cosmetics industry underscores the cultural dynamics of reinvention is through positioning consumers as recipients of the latest scientific breakthroughs and developments in beauty. In this way, the emotional and aesthetic work of bodily reinvention is framed in terms of keeping appearances up-to-date with recognized scientific knowledge. In this connection, advertising focused on beauty creams offering non-invasive alternatives to cosmetic surgery has played an important part in redefining bodily reinvention. Consider, for example, the marketing of skincare products by Rodial, a company that has been spectacularly successful through its representation of the scientific efficacy of high-tech, fast-acting products that result in body recontouring without surgery. Rodial offer consumers hungry to purchase a desirable body a range of options – from "Arm Sculpt" (a product containing "Lipocare" and which promises to "banish bingo wings") to "Boob Job" (which offers an increase of up to half a cup size after 56 days) to "Tummy Tuck" (which can reduce "the abdominal area by up to 2cm in 8 weeks"). Such purported fixes are lifted straight from the cosmetic menus of plastic surgery, a cross-referencing designed to entice consumers. A triumph of hype over substance? There are many who think so, to such an extent that consumer complaints about Rodial led to an investigation by the UK's Advertising Standards Agency in 2011. Even so, the buying of such expensive beauty creams that promise instant transformation remains vast.

In many ways, the cosmetics industry is increasingly dependent for its revenue upon the latest techno-scientific developments in the field of cosmetic plastic surgery. The increasing intrusion of the claims of cosmetic plastic surgery into the marketing of cosmetics is part and parcel of the commercial logics to influence women and men to spend cash on body-maintenance and body-transformation. Again, consider some of the following advertising claims (selected somewhat randomly from fashion magazines) for skin-care products:

- "Surgery can wait! You laugh, you frown, your brow furrows ... your skin contracts and wrinkles deepen. Our solution? Wrinkle De-Crease."
- "Pump it up 40%: Up to 40% Plumper Lips Collagen Effect."
- "Try the latest advances in non-surgical facelift treatment."
- "My Lips Are In Perfect Shape: My Lips Look Fabulously Full and Perfectly Contoured."
- "As good as surgery: airbrushed perfection in an instant."

From the ideological standpoint of such advertising language, it is clear that we live today in a world in which beauty is increasingly intricately interwoven with the aesthetics of cosmetic surgery. From this angle, women (and increasingly men) are rendered "desirable" only to the extent that the *project* of anti-ageing and its marketing-related strategies of reinvention are adopted and followed. Consumer society requires a salutary stiffening of the resolve of individuals: to knuckle down and reverse all signs of ageing, to identify and destroy indications of mortality. In globalized consumer society, these strategies may be many and varied, but they increasingly draw inspiration from and reference cosmetic surgery. This now provides a convenient transition to a more detailed examination of the rise of cosmetic surgery and makeover culture.

Drastic plastic

As an indication that the reinvention impulse of consumer culture goes all the way down – into the very contours of the body – one need only consider the phenomenal rise of cosmetic surgery and related makeover industries. Whilst not as large as either the cosmetics or diet industries, cosmetic surgical culture is both truly global and booming. The total worldwide market for cosmetic surgery and its associated invasive technologies was valued at $35 billion in sales for 2010. If cosmetic surgery represents big business in the twenty-first century, this is partly because of its remarkable proliferation of offerings and diversification in services. Not that long ago cosmetic surgery was essentially synonymous with facelifts (rhytidectomy) or nose jobs (rhinoplasty), and was largely the preserve of the rich and famous. Today cosmetic surgery has also come to mean Botox, breast implants, liposuction, tummy tucks, penile enlargements and thigh and buttock lifts. Moreover there has been a noticeable democratization of cosmetic medicine, with a wholesale shift in the availability of such services to the mass market, often financed on credit cards and personal loans. Hence cosmetic surgical culture is the arrival of an age in which consumers are willing to go into debt to finance their desires for flatter stomachs, bigger breasts and younger looking faces.

What does this tell us about the world we live in? Some critics view the spread of cosmetic surgical culture as symptomatic of the lures of narcissism, of a culture held in thrall to the superficialities of appearance. Cosmetic surgical culture, however, rejects the charge that it is superficial. Nowadays, or at least many advocates of makeover culture argue, appearance and identity are increasingly interwoven; the design of appearance becomes a "project of identity". Yet even if this is so, it is informative if one compares – drawing from figures released by the International Society of Aesthetic Plastic Surgeons – the different kinds of bodily reinvention purchased through cosmetic surgery around the globe. Throughout North America and the UK, breast implants and liposuction are the most popular surgical procedures. (In the US, the American Society for Aesthetic Plastic Surgery estimated that there were 318,123 breast augmentations performed in 2010. In the UK, the British Association of Aesthetic Plastic Surgeons estimated that 9,418 underwent breast augmentations in 2010.) Yet this is not the case in countries such as Japan, China or India, where instead rhinoplasty (nose augmentation) and blepharoplasty (modification of the eyelid) are more common.

The UK's love affair with cosmetic surgical culture has been reflected throughout the early 2000s in the routine doubling of patient numbers requesting surgical procedures (see Elliott 2008). Yet if cosmetic surgical culture brooks large in the UK, its hold is even more dramatic throughout Europe in general. *Time* magazine ran a feature, "Europe's Extraordinary Makeover", which documented unprecedented numbers of individuals demanding elective cosmetic surgery during the early 2000s. Countries such as France, Germany, Spain and Turkey all outstripped Britain in their consumption of the culture of nip and tuck. Interestingly, it is among the younger generation that we find the most passionate embracement of surgical culture.

Cheaper and more widely available than ever before, cosmetic surgery has fast become a lifestyle choice. For good or ill, celebrity culture has been central in this connection, with its novel blending of Botox and bling transforming various aspects of today's cultural landscape. What is under continual review here is the reinvented body. Magazines such as *Who Weekly* and *People*, as well as television programmes such as *E News* and *Entertainment Tonight*, document the surgical enhancements and cosmetic transformations of celebrities. Makeover TV programmes likewise cast the body as a site of transformation and reinvention. Programmes such as American network ABC's *Extreme Makeover* and the UK Channel 4's *Ten Years Younger*, which deployed cosmetic procedures to "redesign" women, as well as various cable offerings including *Cosmetic Surgery Live*, *The Swan* and MTV's *I Want a Famous Face*, show in microscopic detail bodies as pumped, plucked, pummelled, suctioned, stitched, shrunk and surgically augmented. Advanced plastic surgery, high-tech cosmetic enhancements to the body, cosmetic dentistry and novel exercise and diet regimes are routinely used in such programmes to artificially enhance beauty, to resculpt the body and to restructure the self.

If celebrity-inspired cosmetic surgery is a dominant symbol of contemporary culture, this is because it runs all the way down into routine social practices – such that the human body is today increasingly cast as infinitely plastic and pliable. Plasticity is of course good news to mainstream commercial life, and there are few more profitable areas of contemporary consumer culture than where the makeover industries intersect with shopping. The consumer industry and consumer markets undertake continual cross-referencing of products, labels, brands and services to the cosmetic resculpting and reconstructing of the body. The whole commercial language of cosmetic surgical culture is relentlessly focused on episodic change, the purchase of one-off transactions. Cosmetic procedures – from Botox and collagen fillers to liposuction and breast augmentation – are increasingly reduced to a purchase mentality. There's now an emergent generation of consumers who might be called the Plastic Generation, who treat cosmetic surgery as on a par with shopping: consumed fast and with immediate results. Jennifer Hayashi Danns's *Stripped*, an autobiographical account of the culture of lap-dancing clubs, underscores the "instant gratification" connected to the purchase of breast implants. The incessant talk of breast implants in the lap-dancing industry, according to Danns, means that women feel they are purchasing the equivalent of a new car or designer handbag when deciding to go under the surgeon's knife. This is a trend which now percolates throughout the wider culture, especially with breast implants rendered normative through online pornography and reality TV shows.

The reinvention message peddled by cosmetic surgery and the makeover industries is arguably especially ironic. The marketing spin from various makeover industries is that there is nothing to stop you reinventing yourself however you choose. If there are advantages in being able to re-sculpt your body according to your own self-design, however, there are also restrictions. Perhaps most significantly, surgical enhancements of the body are largely fashioned with the short-term in mind. They are, literally, until "the next procedure". Any patient or client returning from a cosmetic procedure performed by a top surgeon in, say, Harley Street London or Beverley Hills is today likely to do so with more than mere bandages and wounds. For many cosmetic surgical institutes now dispatch their patients home with a magazine, catalogue or sometimes DVD – in which is outlined other cosmetic procedures by which one can keep one's surgically enhanced body up-to-scratch. Even so, surgical culture combines brilliant technology with dramatic self-fashioning, medical advances with a narcissistic understanding of the self as a work of art. The current cultural fascination with cosmetic surgery represents the struggle of fantasy against reality, the pyrrhic victory of society over biology.

The explosion in cosmetic surgery currently unfolding holds a mirror to the social logics of reinvention unleashed by globalization, with its blurring of fact and fantasy, culture and biology. Certainly there was a moment in the early 2000s when it looked as though cosmetic surgery and its related makeover culture was about to establish a new orthodoxy as regards beauty and body norms. For a period, a brash new sensibility over-determined by cosmetic surgical culture – and increasingly evident throughout fashion, film, pop music, cosmetics and the like – ruled. But that period has today been brought low, and largely as a result of the excesses of the cosmetic surgical and makeover industries themselves. In 2011, for example, a media scandal erupted concerning ruptures in breast implants made by a French company, Poly Implant Prosthesis (PIP). It emerged that the PIP implants were not made with medical–grade silicone (as required by European law), but rather industrial–grade silicon, which is used for example in the manufacture of mattresses. The scandal linked the faulty implants with cancer, as it emerged that more than 30,000 women in

France had undergone breast implants with industrial silicone. Various public protests unfolded across Europe, and health agencies in France, Germany, the Czech Republic and elsewhere recommended the immediate removal of faulty implants.

In the meantime, as with the bulk of global media scandals, talk of health risks and medical dangers flourished as regards cosmetic surgery. Anti-ageing injections and related facial fillers were linked in 2012 with serious health complications, infections and deformities. Fears about the safety of various non-surgical cosmetic procedures intensified, as did public debate regarding the regulation of unqualified cosmetic practitioners. Such media scandals have also drawn attention to the long-term emotional consequences of the so-called "instant gratifications" of cosmetic surgical culture, as scars and deformities are in turn linked to lives being devastated. Cosmetic surgical culture and the makeover industries, however, remain an extraordinarily powerful influence in contemporary societies, and it is far from clear that media coverage of botched boob jobs and the excesses of unregulated industries is enough to turn the tide on consumer demand for such bodily reinvention. That is to say, the cultural rise and flourishing of cosmetic surgery appears interlocked with our new relations between personal reinvention and social reproduction. Whether such flourishing, which I have tied to new forms of reinvention in the age of accelerated globalization, will tip into a full-blown faltering is an altogether different issue.

2

THE REINVENTION OF PERSONS

Self-reflection and critical self-examination are not qualities most people might associate with parties, but psychologists and psychotherapists who run "speed shrinking parties" apparently thrive on mixing advice and adventure in newfound proportion. Parties of the speed shrinking variety represent a new trend in psychotherapy, one geared to the denizens of a 24/7 media culture in which the desire for fast lifestyles is matched by a desire for quick assessment of any associated emotional problems. In a world of corporate networking, short-term contracts, negotiated intimacies and just-in-time deliveries, the three-minute analytical session offered by speed shrinking is one clearly geared to those seeking reinvention on the run. This is no doubt a central reason for the explosion of interest in fast therapy, which as Susan Shapiro – author of *Speed Shrinking* – notes has taken off "like wildfire".

The rapid-fire therapy dished out at speed shrinking parties, writes Vincent M. Mallozzi in *The New York Times*, consists of "therapists, many sitting behind piles of business cards and books they had written, hoping to achieve chemistry with their new-found clients". Such sought after chemistry, presumably desired as much by the patient (read: client) as the therapist, needs to be mixed in three-minute bursts – for this is a form of therapy in which overshooting the allotted analytic session time equals only thirty seconds. Mallozzi reports from one such speed shrinking party the plight of a middle-aged man worried about the tenure of his job, and increasingly anxious at the prospects of finding himself unemployed. With the clock ticking on the session, the therapist queried whether her client had any fallback skills, or perhaps residual career ambitions. Nothing readily came to mind for the client, although the desire to write a work of fiction is mentioned in passing. As the three-minute deadline approaches, the therapist delivers her fast assessment: "Pursue this new venture. When you are in a situation like this, you must reinvent yourself." Therapy and reinvention, it transpires, go together hand in hand.

In this chapter, elaborating upon the theme of the reinvention of persons, I shall critically examine the rise of therapy and uses of self-help literature. In examining the pervasiveness of therapy in contemporary societies, I shall in the first section of the chapter briefly consider the views of those writers who have suggested that therapy represents an oppressive conformity through the management of people's emotions. Rejecting such evaluations, I want to suggest that therapy should be understood instead as primarily a mechanism of self-reinvention, one increasingly geared to speed and instant change. The second section of the chapter turns to consider the centrality of self-help literature in reconstituting the self today. In the final section I discuss the intricate connections between celebrity culture and reinvention society.

Fast therapy

Ours is the age of therapy. Ever since Sigmund Freud discovered the powers of "the talking cure" – in which the so-called patient speaks to the so-called therapist about whatever comes to mind, freely and without limitation – women and men throughout the expensive, polished cities of the West have sought out the cultivated benefits and diversions of therapy. In this sense, psychoanalysis as a form of therapy has offered people the possibility of alternatives, of different lives. Psychoanalysis shows, among other things, that the emotional lives women and men lead (as well as the emotional lives they do not lead) are open to interrogation, reappraisal and redrafting.

Ours is also the age of therapeutics, especially at the level of the reconstruction and reinvention of the self. The language of therapeutics today reigns supreme, at least throughout the contemporary Western world, for engaging and reflecting on core dilemmas of the self. Anxiety, narcissism, depression, neurosis, phobia, mourning, acting-out, defence-mechanism, compulsion and trauma: the vocabulary of therapeutics has become a central aspect of the emotional scripts through which contemporary women and men engage with the self, others and the wider world.

Finally, and in addition to the pervasiveness of therapy and the language of therapeutics, ours is the age of a wholesale therapy culture. That is to say, the culture of therapy pervades not only the worldview of individuals but also a framework of meaning for companies, organizations, institutions and, indeed, nations and geopolitical regions. Today, and as never before, companies routinely undergo (and seek to recover from) periods of crisis or stress. Organizations and corporations go about the business of "confidence-building", in order to "heal" employee distrust in leadership or management. Entire countries are said to experience periods of "national trauma" – such as the United States after the terror attacks of 9/11 or the United Kingdom after the London riots of 2011. Traumatized national communities are, arguably, part and parcel of a therapeutic imperative which has moved centre stage in the contemporary period.

This overlapping of individual therapy, the language of therapeutics and therapy culture can be found in various sectors of everyday life and popular culture. From the therapist's couch to cybertherapy, from TV talk shows such as *Oprah, Ricki Lake* and *Geraldo,* to confessional autobiographies like Elizabeth Wurtzel's *Prozac Nation*, from life coaching to speed shrinking: the imperative of the talking cure holds sway. Notwithstanding the immense complexities of (as well as the differences between) psychotherapy, psychoanalysis and its related variants, the notion of self-reinvention lies at the core of all such endeavours. Therapy is, from this angle, deeply interwoven with the search for "the New You". An overriding belief in the possibilities of self-reconstruction, redesign and reorganization infuses various versions of individual therapy, but such longings are also marshalled in living rooms across the globe, as a mass-mediated spectacle of private anxieties are dramatized for public consumption. Radio talkback, TV talk-shows and cybertherapy are all at the core of this restructuring of the "talking cure" through the twin forces of multimedia and popular culture.

What accounts for our culture's fascination with therapy? How should we understand the rise of therapy, both its uses at the level of individual psychology and the wider power it exerts at the level of culture? Do therapy and the language of therapeutics represent simply a new form of social control? Some critics have suggested precisely this and, given the attention accorded to such views, it is important to briefly consider these now.

In his influential book of the late 1950s, *The Triumph of the Therapeutic*, Philip Rieff cast the rise of therapy in terms of a rebranding of emotional life, principally with reference to psychological illness. This rebranding involved the therapeutic scrutiny of people's psychology (particularly focusing on personal unhappiness), framed as part of a broader quest for "emotional health". In wider cultural terms, therapy for Rieff seeks to construct "the sane self in a mad world" (1965). Developing upon

Rieff's notion of the triumph of the therapeutic, the American historian Christopher Lasch also criticized therapy, writing of an emergent "culture of narcissism" (1991). According to Lasch, the therapeutic encounter promotes a kind of cultural hypochondria in which individuals turn away from the collective problems of society and retreat narrowly inwards on the self. For Lasch, the spread of a culture of narcissism opens the way for a therapeutic imperative in which crisis becomes both permanent and personalized. More recently, Frank Furedi, in his book *Therapy Culture* (2003), has likewise attacked the dominance of therapy culture, which he claims imposes a new cultural conformity through an oppressive management of people's emotions.

Another critique of the rise of therapy – a more complex and, I think, more interesting one – focuses on its recoding of traditional religious confession for a secular age. One version of this criticism is that developed by the late French historian, Michel Foucault. Foucault's writings, indebted to structural linguistics and post-structuralist theory, are technically dense; the argument I seek to develop here, which draws on but also departs from Foucault, thus involves a somewhat more complex vocabulary than I have used elsewhere in this book. The core of Foucault's argument, bluntly put, is that therapy reorders traditional religious confession as a form of privatism; this it does through "manufacturing" a truth in the ongoing production of stories by which people narrate their lives. From this perspective, individuals are able to access some deeper emotional "truth" about their life through a therapeutic dialogue in which confession (usually confessing to unacceptable sexual desires) is central. Therapy for Foucault is part and parcel of the rise of "confessional society":

> The confession has spread its effects far and wide. It plays a part in justice, medicine, education, family relationships, and love relations, in the most ordinary affairs of everyday

life, and in the most solemn rites; one confesses one's
crimes, one's sins, one's thoughts and desires, one's illnesses
and troubles; one goes about telling, with the greatest
precision, whatever is most difficult to tell.

(1978:59)

In developing this argument Foucault traces a move during
the late nineteenth century in the language of confession away
from the Church and onto the psychoanalyst's couch, where the
worried-well allegedly manufacture new identity truths through
the "talking cure". "In the Californian cult of the self", Foucault
reflected on the rise of therapy culture, "one is supposed to
discover one's true self, to separate it from what might obscure
or alienate it, to decipher its truth thanks to psychological or
psychoanalytic science."

The "talking cure" of therapy for Foucault fits with a whole
gamut of experiences that he calls "technologies of the self".
Like prisons or clinics or hospitals, therapies function to lock
the self within the discourses or scripts of what is considered
appropriate behaviour; we relinquish what we might have
become in order to fit with the scripts of who we are supposed
to be. Foucault sees therapy, or the Californian cult of the self,
as interwoven with the rise of "disciplinary power", in which
discourse circulates to regulate the production of "docile bodies"
(1978).

Foucault's account of technologies of the self, as a critique of
therapy and the psy-professions, has been hugely influential
in the social sciences and humanities. And there is much in this
account which is compelling, as therapy has undoubtedly been
intricately connected with the production of power and the
regulation of behavioural patterns of individuals in modern
societies. That said, there are serious limitations to Foucault's
analysis of the self (see Elliott 2007). Certainly, Foucault's sug-
gestion that therapy has become simply an extension of religious
confession is less than convincing: psychoanalysis, for example,

is premised on the notion of a repressed unconscious, which renders problematic the idea that people can simply "confess" to the secret promptings of desire. But what I want to focus on here, which is equally problematic because Foucault does not focus on this point, concerns the changing ways in which contemporary confessions – or, if you will, therapy – take place in public. I refer to the rise of therapeutic confession in the mass media, but also Web 2.0 and related digital technologies. Had Foucault been able to consider the role of new communication technologies upon the formation and reformation of the self, he might have seen just how powerfully confessional culture constructs new privatized relations – in which, contrary to his sometimes fatalistic account of how power mysteriously operates behind the backs of individuals, the reinvention of self and broader social relations arises as a skilled cultural accomplishment.

Therapy, I am suggesting, is a system of reinvention through which contemporary women and men seek to reconstruct the self. Therapy, at least those versions of it influenced by psychoanalysis and psychotherapeutics, is not just a means to limit or overcome psychological "illnesses" and "trauma" – although its language is often couched in this way. As an expression of the drive to reinvention, therapy seeks to promote the *redesign* of the self as a means of achieving a sense of greater personal autonomy. This is not to say that those engaged in therapeutic endeavours are necessarily successful in achieving greater self-understanding; therapy, as has been well documented in various studies, can sometimes also promote dependence – and in extreme situations might also function as a form of addiction. Yet the general point remains that the goals of therapy are geared to self-reinvention, and thus it should be evaluated as part of a broader technology of reinvention.

Perhaps one of the most intriguing ways in which therapy, understood as a technology of reinvention, has developed in the twenty-first century concerns the radical speeding-up of its delivery time. Consider, for example, the following. In Freud's

Vienna, people committing to psychoanalytic treatment were, in effect, signing up for a programme of self-exploration that might range anywhere from three to five years. Moreover, the slow, emotionally difficult work of therapy would be undertaken on an almost daily basis – typically, three to four days a week over the duration of approximately one hour each session. By contrast, many versions of contemporary therapy centre on quick delivery. Fast therapy, as noted at the beginning of this chapter, has become all the rage. From life coaching to phone therapy, and from cyber-therapy to speed shrinking: therapy today is delivered faster than ever before, with an immediacy to the promise of self-reinvention which is especially striking. In our high-speed society, time has been radically compressed – hence, the spread of fast therapy.

Accompanying this acceleration in the delivery-time of therapy, the contemporary period has also been marked by the spread of therapeutics into more and more sectors of popular culture and everyday life. As a result of Web 2.0, digital culture and new forms of media interaction, the therapeutic ethos has moved well beyond the consulting room and into every facet of daily life. In promoting new forms of therapy as part of a wider system of mediated reinvention, the influence of the talking cure can be tracked at the levels of talkback radio, TV talk-shows and online dialogues. Aspects of popular culture become reorganized in terms of therapeutics, with the imperative to confess (somewhat in the fashion analysed by Foucault) a central theme.

"Ours is a society", writes Susan Sontag, "in which secrets of private life that, formerly, you would have given nearly anything to conceal, you now clamour to get on a television show to reveal" (2004). One reason that the public display of emotion is experienced by growing numbers of women and men as energizing is that therapeutics has gone global – offering to reach new audiences in distant locations. American media theorist Mimi White argues that contemporary popular culture has given a novel twist to therapeutic confession, switching confessional speech away from a singular expert (the therapist) and towards a whole host of possible audiences, including listeners, viewers, hosts, experts and others. "At the heart of the new therapeutic culture", says White, "everyone confesses over and over again to everybody else" (White, 1992: 179). Psychotherapy is only one very particular model advanced by our globalized confessional culture. Twelve-step therapy programmes, personal counselling, memory recovery experts, addiction management programmes, Gestalt and behavioural therapy, phone and cyber-therapy, peer counsellors, Internet analysts: the list of therapies today continually crosses and multiplies, producing hybrids and new techniques and models for public confession.

If living in a mediated therapeutic culture offers new possibilities for the redesign of the self, it is also the case that new burdens arise as well. Many critics of therapy culture are correct, in some part at least, to dismiss aspects of the confessional turn in public life as apolitical or trivial. Arguably the spread of confessional morality has contributed, at least for some individuals, to a retreat from social problems, in a turn towards privatism. Eva Moskowitz, in *In Therapy We Trust*, argues that therapy culture "focuses our attention on the private life, blinding us to the larger, public good" (2001:7). Moskowitz's standpoint is interesting, but needs to be recast in order to adequately grasp how therapeutics intersects with reinvention society. Confessional culture, to be sure, can promote a narrowing of the arts of public political life, but not necessarily. The public confession of private sentiments can, in fact, work the other way around – opening out of the self to an increasingly interconnected world and thus promoting self-reinvention.

The seductions of self-help

These days, when we are not being bombarded with advertising and promotions for the reinvention of self, we are being told that the self is a site for endless improvement. Once again, the psychological sciences figure prominently in this cultural under-writing of the arts of self-improvement. Psychoanalysis, psychotherapy and related discourses of self-investigation loom large in contemporary mappings of our relationship to ourselves. In an age which dethrones the power of expert knowledge, however, the role of therapist has been largely outsourced, passed over to the actual customers of self-improvement and self-reinvention. In this shift from expert (therapist) to customer (patient), we find the commercial logics of do-it-yourself. Enter the self-improvement industry, inclusive of everything from 12-step recovery programmes to life coaching, and its dazzling techniques for "self-help".

From one angle, the rise of self-help represents the con-temporary search for balance between secure self-identity on the one hand and experimental reinvention on the other. It is a feature of global capitalism that advancement, progress and the future are all represented as more or less synonymous with a complete break from the past; the established patterns of custom, habit or routine are of apparently little value for contemplating the novel challenges and risks of tomorrow, let alone those of the day after. The modern age instead delivers choice, and as never before. We cherish choice as promotional of self-flourishing and freedom, while believing we are free agents capable of making autonomous choices among an indefinite range of possible goods and services. Ironically, this very com-plex diversity of choices – a world in which there is no choice but to choose – confronts the individual as overwhelming. And it is this cultural contradiction from which the launching of self-help proceeds.

The genre of self-help literature, the explosive popularity of which has served to bolster an otherwise faltering publishing industry, fulfils various reinvention functions. To begin with, self-help literature is a kind of overall lifestyle reinvention, largely dismissive of the past (even when proclaiming its importance) and in love with the prospect of future possibilities.

All that was past – family upbringing, childhood experiences, significant intimate relationships, established cognitive frames of reference – transforms to an "open future". In this sense, the genre of self-help underwrites the changeability of persons and things. The literature of self-help, broadly speaking, proclaims that identities can be shucked off, recast, other identities tried on for size and then profligately performed throughout the theatres of social life until such time as the self's identity demands further reshuffling. In the midst of a world of perpetual global change, the genre of self-help reassuringly consoles of the availability of potential alternative lives and lifestyles.

Self-help, too, for all its crass commercialism, is intricately interwoven with reinvention in a more strategic sense. Like the reinvented "new you" which the genre promises, self-help offers various tools of reinvention as a means of preparing for the attainment of a desired lifestyle. This is what the British sociologist Anthony Giddens calls "strategic life-planning" or "life-plan calendars" (1991:85). Strategic life-planning centres on an adherence to certain timing devices for the realization of lifestyle change desired by the individual, and Giddens argues that self-help literature makes clear the importance of preparing for the future in a world which is increasingly post-traditional in orientation. Such timing devices, or tools of reinvention, offered by self-help literature range from, say, programmes of self-writing (the keeping of a journal, or autobiography) to five easy steps for taking charge of one's life. Understanding that the individual is responsible for the building and re-building of life-plan calendars, and that persons must continuously engage in the making of their identities, is a pervasive feature of the self-help genre. Self-help, on this view, is essentially an endeavour of reinvention.

It is, though, and perhaps above all, speed that counts most in the negotiation of self-help today. We live, as Milan Kundera brilliantly put it, in a culture of "pure speed" (1995:1) – where lines of flight from person to person, organization to

organization, at once proliferate and intensify. This is well illu-
strated, for example, by considering self-help books currently on
the market. Title after title underscores how the time/space
architecture of our lives is driven by the pressures of pure speed.
The 4 Hour Body, *34 Instant Stress Busters*, *Instant Self-Confidence*,
Fast Road to Happiness: these are just some of the books currently
available to women and men seeking to refashion, restructure
and rebuild their personal lives. But, as I say, professional life
is also ripe for a menu of continual instant change. *1 Hour
Negotiator*, *30 Minute Career Fast Track Kit*, *Fast Thinking*, *Fast
Track to the Top* and *The Attention Deficit Workplace*: professionals
the world over are busy remaking and reorganizing their careers
on the pure speed model promoting the faster, quicker, lighter.

In this emergent cultural fantasy tailored for the twenty-first
century, professionalism turns into performance, presentation and
public relations. The mantra runs as follows: just as there are
no constraints on the individual self, so there are no natural
limits to promoting speed in one's personal and professional life.

Celebrity culture: reinvention as public obsession

Celebrity is at once astonishingly mesmerizing and mind-
numbingly dull, crazily libertarian and depressingly conformist.
Our culture of celebrity feigns the new, the contemporary, the
up-to-date, as it recycles the past. Celebrities are constantly on
the brink of obsolescence, of appearing out of date. Today Lady
Gaga, yesterday Beyoncé, the day before Madonna. Celebrities
are radically excessive in this respect: in a world teeming with
images and information, celebrities trade in sheer novelty as a
means of transcending the fame of others with whom they
compete for public renown. To a large extent, celebrity represents a central driving force behind the cascade of our reinvention society.

The conduit of celebrity arises, in sociological terms, from
massive institutional changes throughout the West, involving

a wholesale shift from industrial manufacture to a post-industrial economy orientated to the finance, service, hi-tech and communications sectors. As the economy becomes cultural as never before, ever more dependent on media, image and public relations, so personal identity comes under the spotlight and open to revision. The new economy, in which the globalization of media looms large, celebrates both technological culture and the power of new technologies to reshape the order of things. The current cultural obsession with the remaking and transformation of the self is reflective of this, and arguably nowhere more so than in the attention that popular culture lavishes upon celebrity. The relentless media scrutiny of the private lives of celebrities – especially the shape, size, exercise regimes, addictions, recoveries, cures, cosmetic enhancements and surgical alterations of celebrity bodies – runs all the way from paparazzi and gossip magazines to entertainment news and YouTube.

In any case, today's celebrity-led recasting of reinvention is pitched on an altogether different terrain to yesteryear's notions of fame. The historian Leo Braudy, in his pioneering study *The Frenzy of Renown* (1997), contends that the era of Hollywood and its invention of glamorous film stars served to personalize fame, with public renown arising as a result of such factors as personal uniqueness, artistic originality or individual creativity. Fame, in a sense, was tied to genius. From Laurence Olivier's dramatic talents to Rudolf Nureyev's ballet grace, from Groucho Marx's comic mastermind to John Lennon's pop virtuosity: fame was primarily cast in the sense of value, art, innovation and tradition. Yet such an understanding of public renown has, to a large extent, fallen on hard times today. Thanks to technological advances and the spread of digital culture, the terrain of public renown has migrated from Hollywood-inspired definitions of fame to multi-media driven forms of celebrity. This has involved a very broad change from narrow, elite definitions of public renown to more open, inclusive understandings. This is a shift, in effect, from the Hollywood blockbuster to Reality TV, from lifelong stardom to 15 minutes of public renown, and from pop music to *Pop Idol*.

Reinvention comes into its own in this context. If fame was about the cultivation of talent, artistry and originality, celebrity embraces instead the inauthentic, performance, pastiche and parody. What powers the careers of celebrities today is change, disjuncture, trauma and transformation. In a world that has less and less time for long-term commitments and durable relationships, continual reinvention has become a normative part of the field of celebrity. Indeed, how celebrities undertake the reinvention of their private lives has today become a public obsession. From media reports of the drug hell of Amy Winehouse to rumours about Rihanna's latest super-fast diet, from gossip about the marriage of Angelina Jolie and Brad Pitt to the alleged drug habits of Nicole Richie, the stable regimen of magazines such as *OK* and *People* concerns transformations in the private lives of public figures.

To speak of the fast shifting terrain of celebrity may be to speak too hastily. After all, celebrity may look light and liquid when we consider *X Factor* or *Pop Idol*, but such ephemerality is hardly the case for Robert De Niro or The Rolling Stones. Thus it might be a mistake to believe that long-term fame has been completely eclipsed by short-term celebrity, even if the latter has undeniably made inroads into the former in the era of reinvention society. But perhaps such dualism is misleading. Perhaps like most forms of popular culture, the powers and limits of reinvention are deeply interwoven with the production and marketing of celebrities in a deeper sense too. Consider, for example, Oprah Winfrey – who, having retired in 2011 from American daytime television after 25 years in the business, could hardly be described as a stopgap celebrity. The high priestess of change-your-life TV, Winfrey's departure from the circuit of celebrity was globally mourned as an exit of a unique, gifted individual. Her retirement was of course surely that, but also – and perhaps equally interestingly – a fascinating insight into what our culture values in these early decades of the twenty-first century.

Novelist Ian McEwan has written of daytime confessional TV as "the democrat's pornography" (1987), and there can be little doubt that Winfrey lifted this art to the second power. In her book *Oprah: The Gospel of an Icon* (2011), Yale academic Kathryn Lofton writes of Winfrey's "confessional promiscuity" – the daytime television talkfest by which people willingly submit to their personal makeovers in front of millions of viewers and from which they adopt new identities. It is the zoning of makeover or reinvention, I suggest, that takes us to the heart of brand "Winfrey". One of America's richest women, Oprah is estimated to be worth in excess of $US1.5 billion. Winfrey's life story – of a girl who pulled herself up by her own bootstraps and made it on the global media stage – is one her audience has enthusiastically embraced in the form of escape from anxiety over getting stuck in the land of nowhere. Winfrey's key message – "you can reinvent yourself however you so choose" – is music to the ears of contemporary women and men seeking to embrace the therapeutic mantra of flexible reinvention.

The Winfrey brand, in short, fits hand in glove with today's pursuit of endless reinvention, continual change, breakneck speed and a short-termist mentality. Oprah's change-your-life TV dealt this out in spades, and this is obviously one reason her retirement generated such high levels of global media attention. But, significantly, her absence will only be missed temporarily, for our culture of reinvention, serviced by the celebrity preachers of instant therapeutics, is everywhere on the rise.

3

THE REINVENTION OF CAREERS

"Reinventing your self in the 21st century", writes career-life coach Darrell Andrews, "is no longer an option, it is required". Andrews, also known throughout professional circles in the USA as "Coach D", captures the normative demands of career reinvention thus:

> In order to be valuable to corporations, governments and other employers, people must become creative thinkers and innovators as well as upgrade their current skills ... It is quite obvious to anyone who analyzes labor trends, the only way to remain workforce competitive is to possess a skill that is significant to the employer and regularly upgrade that skill set to make your position relevant.
>
> *(Andrews 2011)*

Career and security thus, in the brave new world arising after jobs-for-life, operate at cross-purposes. Notice that Andrews writes of the imperative to "regularly upgrade" skills, an upgrading which even when undertaken is no guarantee of job security (as workplace "guarantees" have gone the way of "lifetime careers"). Whilst a career used to denote the long-term, it is now increasingly about the recombination of skills to move between job functions, departments or industries in the search for some provisional, always short-lived, job security. Hence, the short-term, episodic and fast-paced measures advanced by Coach D in his six-step programme for twenty-first century career reinvention:

1. Participate in trainings designed to identify and mobilize your unique gifts, talents and abilities.
2. Identify a career and life coach who will direct and inspire you through the career transition process.
3. Consider going back to school (or to school if never attended) and learning a new trade-career.
4. Use social networking tools such as LinkedIn to make connections with new career opportunities and networks. LinkedIn has thousands of innovative job and career networking opportunities and it is a free source.
5. Identify how your passion connects to hot job markets such as green jobs, technology and healthcare.
6. Develop a network of people who can help you advance in your career. Ask for their advice often.

The reinvention of careers it transpires, much like everything else in the era of reinvention society, favours instant changes, quick fixes and instantaneous connections.

This chapter turns to focus on the reinvention of self required of contemporary women and men – no matter what age or skill set – for the jobs they seek, need or desire. The first section of the chapter explores the wider socio-economic contexts of career reinvention through contextualizing the rise of the new "project economy" – in which endless rounds of job cutting, outsourcing and financial crisis reign supreme. The second section of the chapter turns to consider how professionals undertake career makeovers in an institutional context of workplace reinvention.

The project-based economy

Ours is the era of transnational corporations, global electronic outsourcing, just-in-time deliveries, the automation of jobs, corporate lay-offs and multiple rounds of job cutting. The term "globalization" has become a kind of cultural shorthand for capturing these tumultuous socio-economic changes, and – whilst the debate over globalism has been widespread in the social sciences – it is widely agreed that globalization has given rise to the emergence of a "new economy" in which financialization, communications and services come to the fore in the polished, expensive cities of the West.

The impact of multinational corporations, able to export industrial production to low-wage spots around the globe, and to restructure investment in the West away from manufacture to the finance, service and communications sectors, has spelt major changes in the ways people live their lives, how they approach work, as well as how they position themselves within the employment marketplace. Whilst employment has become much more complex than in previous periods as a result of the acceleration of globalization, one key institutional fact redefining the contemporary condition has been the rapid decline of lifetime employment. The end of a job-for-life, or of a career developed within a single organization, has been interpreted by some critics as heralding the arrival of a "new economy" – flexible, mobile, networked. Global financier and philanthropist George Soros argues that "transactions" now substitute for "relationships" in the modern economy.

Reference to the "new economy" has become a stereotype within recent discussions of globalization, and I want to clarify its meaning here – as I am going to subsequently suggest that a better term is the "project-based economy", a term especially relevant for grasping the widespread trend towards career reinvention. The new economy, as referenced by economists and sociologists especially, refers to the emergence of computer-based production technology, largely in the service, finance and communication sectors; the spread of new information technologies, which underpin spatially dispersed global production and consumption; and new ways of organizing work, primarily around the imperatives of adaptability and flexibility.

All of these features of the new economy have spelt rapid change throughout both public and private life, and arguably nowhere more so than in people's fears over their professional self-worth, the splintering of personal identity and the fragmentation of family life. Indeed, it is in the shift from the traditional work contract (long-term job security, orderly promotions, longevity-linked pay and pensions) to the new work deal (short-term contracts, job hopping and options shopping, high risk-taking) that a new kind of economy nests. This is what I shall call the "project-based economy", one in which professionals move from a world of "lifetime careers" to a world of "project-based assignments". Robert Reich, Chancellor's Professor of Public Policy at the University of California, Berkeley, captures well the new marketplace logics of project-based work: "It's a spot auction market. What you're paid is what you're worth at that particular time" (in Warshaw 2011).

I mentioned earlier that globalization plays a key role in the emergence of the new project-based economy, and it is worth considering a little further how globalism penetrates deeply into the economy and restructures employment and working life. For this is an especially important point for grasping why and how the reinvention of careers has moved to centre-stage in professional life in our own time. Some writers have argued that time – specifically, a new and different conception of the temporal conditions of social life – is of key significance in this connection. Over a period since the Second World War, according to this argument, a faith in the durability of social relationships and trust in social and economic institutions has weakened. Experience – the idea that things, including human beings, develop and mature over time – has been sidelined, replaced instead with a focus on the here-and-now of the moment. The central institutional force driving this shift in perceptions of time is globalization. The culture of globalization, as the American sociologist Richard Sennett puts it, is that of acute "short-termism" (1998). It is not just that social life is speeding up with the technological advances unleashed by globalization, nor that people are often in a great hurry to do things and live life to the fullest. It is rather that contemporary women and men now calculate that things – including human relationships – do not last for long. Short-term thinking increasingly takes precedence over long-term planning – not only in politics, but in the workplace too. Authors such as Sennett see the flexibility demanded of workers by multinational corporations as demonstrating the corrosive power of globalization, promoting a dominant conception of individuals as dispensable, even ultimately disposable. And it is against this backdrop of globalism that Sennett cites statistics showing that average American college graduates today can expect in their lifetime to hold 12 positions or posts, plus they will be required to change their skills base at least three times. From this viewpoint, yesteryear's job-for-life is replaced today by short-term contract work.

If downsizing, flexibility and job insecurity have become the mark of our times, how might this influence how women and men think about their working lives? How do such economic changes impinge upon people's sense of professional identity? And how might the building of a long-term successful career be pursued in a world devoted to the short-term? Let me return briefly to Sennett's arguments about the rise of the imperatives of flexibility and risk-taking in the globalizing world of work. Sennett's contention, bluntly put, is that we have moved from a work world of rigid, hierarchical organizations, in which self-discipline shaped the durability of the self, to a brave new economy of corporate re-engineering, innovation and risk, in which demands for employment flexibility move to the fore.

According to Sennett, the rise of flexible capitalism – however much flexibility and risk-taking are said to give people more freedom to shape the direction of their professional and personal lives – actually leads to crushing new burdens and oppressions. Flexible capitalism is "flexible" only in as far as its workers and consumers accept the dictates of a post-hierarchical world, accept that it is they, and they alone, who must strive to be ever-more flexible, and accept the abandonment of traditional models of work as well as standard definitions of success. This is a redefinition of success away from past achievements, as reflected in the professional résumé, and towards future flexibility and readiness to embrace change. This is, in short, makeover culture lifted to the spheres of work and employment.

When people are inserted into a world of detachment and superficial co-operativeness, of weak ties and interchangeable relationships, and when all this is shaped by the pursuit of risk-taking and self-reinvention, the hold of traditional ways of doing things radically diminishes. This can be potentially liberating: employees find new thrills and spills in redefining work identities and creating fluid and innovative working relationships. But there is also something more unsettling at work. A working life that is fashioned largely through episodic encounters and short-term projects has little emotional consistency; and it is this drift of character, of the "corrosion of character", that Sennett fixes his attention firmly upon. According to Sennett, as the coherent working narrative breaks down, so does the symbolic texture of the self. In the 24/7 world of advanced globalization, the durability of a career is replaced by a kind of supermarket experience of the working life – an assemblage of scraps, random desires, chance encounters, the accidental and the fleeting. The fast, short-term, techy culture of globalization is unleashing – it is being suggested – a new paradigm of self-making in work and employment. In a world of short-term contracts, endless downsizings, just-in-time deliveries and multiple careers, the capacity to change and reinvent oneself is fundamental. A faith in flexibility, plasticity and incessant reinvention – all this means we are no longer judged on what we have done and achieved; we're now judged on our flexibility, on our readiness for personal makeover.

How does this brave new corporate world of short-termism affect professional identities? Acclaimed sociologist Zygmunt Bauman provides some useful observations in this connection, particularly in his underscoring of the increasing fragility and liquidity of fears, anxieties and troubles that beset contemporary women and men. In his provocative book *Wasted Lives* (2004) Bauman contends that the key anxiety of the twenty-first century is that of the fear of disposability. This is the fear people today have of being dumped, dropped, displaced, discarded and disowned. Bauman's contention speaks to the fear women and men have today of retrenchment, which can often come at a moment's notice. This is an idea that captures the very troubling anxieties that workers face in a world in which transnational corporations move operations to other countries, literally overnight. And it is an idea that scoops up many contemporary fears concerning global electronic off-shoring, outsourcing and other new forms of technological change.

Bauman's underscoring of the fear of disposability obviously chimes with a world of intensive globalization and expanding mobilities, of instant communications and of enforced mass migrations. Yet whatever the precise adequacy of this social diagnosis, I now want to argue that Bauman's contention concerning fear of disposability sheds light on new social forces motivating people to demand instant self-reinvention through career makeovers.

Career makeovers

Terms such as "flexible futures" and "liquid lifestyles" speak to the big social changes of the era – namely, globalization – and its shakeup of contemporary organizational life. But they also capture a new set of anxieties – some profoundly troubling fears – that beset contemporary women and men as they seek to negotiate the new conditions of work and employment in the early years of the twenty-first century. In societies of reinvention where image rules, where beauty, youth and sex appeal trump most claims to self-sufficiency or knowledge, it is perhaps not surprising that there is a corresponding spotlight on employees' image development and presentation skills. We are speaking about, in short, the commercialization of employee appearance. We are speaking about the lengths that women and men will go to in undertaking career makeovers in order to keep pace with the logics of business and the marketplace today.

Consultants, image advisors, life coaches, career counsellors, beauty and fashion guides: this is part of the new cultural landscape in which work and employment are conducted today. Employers now place an ever-spiralling value on employees' appearance and presentation, and with that, failure to live up to many of today's cruelly demanding employment ideals, resulting in job failure or termination. Workplace success is, among other things, about image, self-marketing and makeover. Dress, deportment, voice and body shape are all sized up – usually implicitly, though increasingly explicitly as well – in today's job market. And wresting success from failure against such an employment backdrop has become more and more about demonstrating a willingness for adaptability, flexibility and change.

This is where workplace makeover really comes into its own, with its vocabulary of voluntaristic clichés drawn straight from American popular culture: "there's still room at the top", "the sky is the limit", "you can make of yourself whatever you want". The will to "make oneself" – to pick oneself up by the bootstraps and get on with things – has, in our own time, become the mantra that you can remake, remould or refashion yourself however you so choose. For corporate culture, jobs (contract, team based, short-term) are fashioned out of such strenuously self-affirmative processes of reconstruction, recalibration and remoulding. If the new economy promises jobs with full flexibility, short-term contracts and innovative work environments, it is also delivers this with an unprecedented level of layoffs, outsourcing, age discrimination and job insecurity. Education qualifications and work experience are all very well, but in the new economy such matters are often sidelined to the more pressing issues of detecting early signs of grey hair or the onset of wrinkled frowns.

Women and men can, of course, seek to shrug off such pressures of our reinvention society. One can be ironic about social trends and fads of beauty, but this does not necessarily weaken their hold upon people. As it happens, the social sciences have been quick to label the emergence, rise and devastating consequence of this presentational culture in the workplace as "lookism". The argument, briefly put, is that "lookism" is a new kind of racism, and one that is sweeping the West today. Here is economist Daniel Hamermesh on the impact of lookism: "My research shows being good-looking helps you earn more money, find a higher-earning spouse and even get better deals on mortgages" (in Salkeld 2011). No wonder, then, that more and more people seek reinvention as a means of coping with the socio-economic imperialism of "lookism". Increasingly women and men, if they have to choose, would rather engage with reinvention society and its makeover culture than suffer the cruel discrimination of "lookism".

If the prospects of reinvention in the workplace then can be represented as consoling, there is at least no shortage of role-models and experts showing how to achieve a better physical appearance and level of presentation at work. In Chapter 1, I argued that consumerism and celebrity culture represent some of the core drivers for cosmetic surgery and the makeover industries throughout contemporary societies. But the rise and flourishing of cosmetic surgery also raise questions about new forms of self-design and self-improvement in the workplace context, which shopping and fame have less to say about. Why is cosmetic surgery, for example, increasingly rife within the corporate world? How has cosmetic surgery become culturally synonymous with a personal readiness for change, adaptability and flexibility? In a previous book, *Making The Cut: How Cosmetic Surgery is Transforming Our Lives* (2008), I set out to investigate the complex, contradictory reasons people have for going under the surgeon's knife. After several years of interviewing patients and surgeons in various parts of the globe, I found what is especially interesting in the surge of liposuction converts and Botox addicts is the social composition of those undergoing drastic plastic. Middle-class professionals and executives are, more and more, turning to cosmetic surgery in an effort to retain, or sometimes acquire, youthful looks. Skilled global professionals – from Sydney to Singapore to San Francisco – are electing for cosmetic surgical procedures in order to maintain a career edge in the rough and tumble of today's fast-changing global economy.

In this new economy of endless downsizings, short-term contracts, just-in-time deliveries and multiple careers, what seems secure today can alter overnight. Jobs are no longer "for life", least of all corporate executive posts. And as men and women adjust to the volatility of the global economy, they also seek out new forms of self-reinvention, in order to try to keep pace with the sheer scale of change. From this angle, the combined forces of globalization, digital information technologies and the new economy are spawning experiments in living, as women and men seek to reinvent their bodies and thus improve their socio-economic prospects. Indeed, cosmetic surgery is widely understood as securing a career-edge for those in search of new, refashioned looks. There is, it should be noted, no single ideal of beauty at work here, however much media images of sex, youth and glamour dominate popular culture. The central desirable terrain is instead that of *revising* one's looks, *changing* appearance, *transforming* the body. Perhaps this is why executives and middle-class professionals are turning to cosmetic surgery to update their looks, in much the same way as a résumé is reorganized. Certainly this is brought out, for example, in an American study which found that 81 per cent of Americans with a net worth of more than $10 million intend to undergo cosmetic surgery in the short-term future.

There is, however, an even deeper relation between commerce and the cosmetic that is worth briefly noting. Cosmetic surgery is, among other things, an act of self-transformation: the surgically enhanced body is one connected to professional and socio-economic success on various levels. The enhancements of cosmetic surgery provide for a kind of success, however, that is future-orientated. Contrary to the adage that track record or past achievement is the best indicator of future possibilities; cosmetic surgical culture is a world in which people are increasingly judged on their willingness to embrace reinvention, their adaptability for makeover. Flexibility, plasticity, liquidity, incessant reinvention: these are the criteria to determine whether a person, especially an employee, might flourish or not. Certainly this holds true at more senior levels of professional life, in which flagging careers have been reversed through cosmetic procedures – as these examples from the UK's *Financial Times* indicate:

- A vice-president who, at the age of 60, was retrenched. Unable to find a new position, and convinced that he was being discriminated against because of his older appearance, he underwent a face-lift. He was appointed to a new vice-presidential position in a large company two months following the surgery.
- A 45 year old female executive in California, who felt that her authority within the company was being eroded by an

energetic younger woman. After the executive underwent procedures for a facelift and eye surgery, the younger woman ceased to pose a threat.

Yet if a willingness to undertake frequent cosmetic procedures is read as reflective of an open, dynamic orientation to the future, this is a mindset that pervades not only the upper echelons of corporate life but also middle-management, the working masses as well as those looking for work but currently cast at the margins of the global economy. Whether buying Botox, consulting a cosmetic image advisor, or perhaps simply consuming cosmetics that are marketed with reference to the latest technological advances in cosmetic surgery, the makeover industries seek to persuade us that human bodies are flawed and pliable, defective and malleable.

Does this mean, then, that employees are the world over increasingly reinventing their selves, presentational skills, résumés and careers in order to fit with the new economic imperatives of the global economy? Perhaps so, at least if organizations, companies and corporations are understood as somehow standing over and above the staff they hire and fire. But it may be too hasty to see organizations and corporations as uncontaminated by the logics – the gains, stresses and strains – of reinvention society. It is possible instead to see companies and corporations – institutional life, if you will – as deeply enmeshed in the very logics of reinvention that they demand of their employees. This provides a convenient transition to the next chapter, which moves from the reinvention of individual careers to the reinvention of corporations.

4

THE REINVENTION OF CORPORATIONS

Is globalization breeding new forms of corporate reinvention? In the age of a globalized planet, the fate of businesses, companies and corporations is performed and negotiated on a global stage; and it is on this global stage that the conditions and consequences of reinvention are produced. "Companies", write Scott D. Anthony and Michael Putz in *Forbes* (2009), "are increasingly recognizing that today's turbulent times require nothing short of continual reinvention. Weathering today's storm isn't enough. Companies have to develop repeatable processes that regularly renew their firms before the next crisis hits".

There are indeed valid reasons to suppose that the development of "repeatable processes that regularly renew" has become the only corporate game in town, and any failure to measure up to this new gold standard is likely to be judged by stockholders and markets as generating risks and problems. Reinvention is revealed as an intensely economic imperative from this angle, and no firm or corporation – no matter how seemingly successful – should cast itself as immune from the ongoing requirements of redesigning, rebranding, refinancing or changing its business model. Just think, for instance, of Borders or Blockbuster – two illustrations of once highly successful companies rendered antiquated, and literally overnight, by the digital communications revolution.

Today's corporate obsession with "repeatable processes that regularly renew" takes us into the heart of globalization, and particularly into the worldwide corporate impacts of outsourcing, offshoring, downsizing, Just in Time deliveries, the emergence of ultra-low cost competitors and collapsing barriers to entry. None of this is news that remains news, and certainly the debate over globalization has been well rehearsed at the levels of business, finance and the broader public sphere. Yet, so familiar are we with the message that globalization spells endless reinvention that it is all too easy to lose sight of the ubiquity of the reinvention programme in corporate life and multinational companies today.

Metamorphosis rules, as companies such as Borders seek to transform into Amazon, or Blockbuster into Netflix, closing old-fashioned retail shops and going into digital delivery. But the new metamorphosis model is about much more than the reorganization of balance-sheets, closing of unprofitable chain stores, refinancing and reappraisal of existing business models. It concerns rather the creation of value through the practices of reinvention itself, as companies, firms and organizations are refashioned to demonstrate to the market an in-built flexibility for the future. Hence, British supermarket giant Tesco announced in 2011 plans to generate an additional one billion pounds of revenue through reinvention initiatives ranging from banking to mobile phones. Consumer company Proctor and Gamble likewise has sought to add five billion pounds in five years from new initiatives and novel markets. And in the USA, Cisco Systems has shifted forcefully into new terrains – ranging from bringing Web 3.0 to China to installing routers in space – and seeking along the way to increase its $40 billion turnover by 25 per cent in five years.

An emergent corporate faith in the powers of plasticity is evidenced by the huge numbers of businesses, firms and companies undertaking endless reinventions of their organizational cultures, markets and products. The reinvention ideal required in new institutions is sometimes dazzlingly asserted and advanced. This is especially true in various sectors of the new economy, especially global finance, high technology and new service firms. The Finnish communications multinational Nokia, for example, embodies this ideology of organizational re-fashioning. Engaged in the manufacturing of mobile devices for the convergent communications and Internet industries, the Nokia Corporation employs staff in 120 countries and has achieved global annual revenues of over 50 billion Euros with sales in more than 150 countries. Yet this telecommunications giant actually began life as a paper manufacturer, and subsequently expanded into rubber works and the manufacture of galoshes; it was not until the 1960s that the company moved into electronics, and then subsequently in the 1970s into telecommunications. Today, in the early years of the twenty-first century, the grip of an imagination for reinvention continues as Nokia refashions itself away from mobile phones and towards mobile devices.

The story of the reinvention of Nokia – from paper manufacturer to communications giant – is spectacular. So too has been its fall from the top. In 2010, the company announced a 40 per cent drop in profits, arising largely as a result of Apple's ascendency in the smart-phone market. But the institutional changes associated with reinvention are not fixed. Indeed, the recent history of organizations suggests that reinvention is constantly unfolding. As Jerry Wind and Alfred West, Jr. write in "Reinventing The Corporation":

> The firm must design and implement any number of programs and associated processes which force the organization

to aspire to new heights and which require for their achievement a rethinking and re-engineering of current practices. ... The reinvention process involves massive individual and organizational change that must be backed by leaders at all levels of the organization. Our training must prepare the firm for change that has no end.

(1991:75)

The diagnosis offered by Wind and West underscores the extent to which corporate life today is continually metamorphosing. In the previous organizational era of hierarchical, producer-driven companies and solid bureaucratic management, the achievement of some degree of fixity was regarded as essential for traversing the turbulent business world; the routines of organizational life were thus regarded as comforting. In today's organizational era of flat, consumer-driven companies and liquid team management, established corporate ways of doing things – habits, if you will – are destroyed and reconfigured at an astonishing rate.

The repertoires of corporate reinvention

The emergence of ongoing corporate restructuring takes us to the core of the new economy, and particularly illustrative of such trends as the American technology giant Cisco Systems. This global technology supplier of hardware such as routers and switches, which directs traffic through Internet networks, briefly attained the status in early 2000 of the world's most valued company – with a market capitalization of $US550 billion. Twelve months later, following the tech-wreck, its stock-market value crashed to $US100 billion. The company was able to survive the worst of this economic downturn, largely because as the world's "Internet plumber" the selling of such network gear remained assured.

Yet Cisco rapidly adapted to the fast-changing circumstances of Web 2.0, quickly cementing its reputation as a cutting-edge corporation at the level of innovation and reinvention. Realizing that its core markets centred on routing and switching had matured, the company branched out into a range of other business opportunities – from Internet telephony to wireless products to optical networks. This expansion of Cisco paid off, and by the late 2000s the company employed more than 66,000 people and had revenues near $40 billion.

What was most striking about this branching out at Cisco from the networking market and into consumer territory was a remarkable change in the whole vocabulary and cognitive frame of the company. Under the direction of chairman and chief executive John Chambers, Cisco appeared to abandon its set ways of doing business, embracing instead a new flexibility, fluidity and adaptability. The strength of Cisco, according to Chambers, derived from its "stretching" into different market directions. To convey the new rules of this corporate strategy and the logic of expansion at Cisco, Chambers indicated that the company no longer stood for "command and control" but instead a new world of "coordination and cultivation". This was less an "engineered" model of management, and more an institutional realm of networks, coalitions and teams. That is to say, the "stretching" of Cisco – which intensified dramatically under the leadership of Chambers – resulted in a range of institutional innovations such as outsourcing and acquisitions. In practice, this saw Cisco move into such markets as virtual health care, cloud computing, routers in space and Internet security. By late 2009, Chambers revealed that Cisco had developed more than 30 "market adjacencies".

If some corporate reinvention is geared to product and market refashioning, some other companies extend the remodelling principle all the way down to the very fabric of organizational structure – and perhaps nowhere is this better dramatized than at Cisco. As it happens, Cisco had long been a corporate innovator. Not only manufacturing, but research and development had been substantially outsourced, as the company acquired various networking firms and integrated them. Yet Cisco's phenomenal reorganization during the 2000s consisted of much more than new acquisitions and outsourcing. Chambers was widely acknowledged by the business and financial world as raising the following thorny questions: can companies reinvent their organizational structure in the same way they rebrand their products and services? Might the organizational model come to resemble the flexibility increasingly demanded of consumer products? What happens if management becomes co-operative?

Chambers answered positively to all of the above, and instigated a sweeping reinvention of Cisco's organizational model in the process. In doing so, he swept away the company's previously functional structure, in which management was divided across domains of engineering, manufacturing and marketing. The very idea of a collaborative organizational culture for Chambers demanded something less bureaucratic, less stifling. Following this train of thought, it became clear to Chambers that the ongoing reinvention of consumer products and services was something that needed to be replicated at the level of co-operative management. This was the notion of a management as a "work in progress". To achieve this, Cisco set up an elaborate matrix of committees comprising managers from various sectors of the company. The committees were divided into two kinds: "Boards" were charged with identifying new markets that might reach $US1 billion; "Councils" with identifying new markets that could reach $US10 billion (*Economist* 2009). Both committees were serviced by "working groups". In 2010, Cisco were unable to calculate how many working groups existed throughout the company, such was the fast assembly and even faster disassembly of these structures in the context of fashioning, responding to and coping with new global markets.

Choosing the reinvention option prompted by global economic imperatives has an intoxicating and multiplying consequence of its own: the more reinvention is deployed as a mantra, the more self-perpetuating and self-intensifying the strategy becomes. At Cisco this much was evident from the rapid spread of "market adjacencies", fast assembly/disassembly of working groups, boards and councils, as well as the wholesale recalibration of its organizational model as a "work in progress". What the label of reinvention doesn't capture, however, is just how far down the forces driving employees at Cisco to reorganize, restructure and rethink their work practices, actually went. Cisco's reinvention of its business model for corporate travel is highly illustrative. Following the global financial crisis of 2008, and coupled to Chambers's directive that the company needed to reduce carbon emissions for travel by 20 per cent, Cisco devised a new travel policy designed to save the company millions of dollars annually. Initially senior management requested employees not to travel across cities for internal company meetings if possible, and at the same time set about planning a complete overhaul of Cisco's global corporate travel.

To do this, Cisco appointed Susan Lichtenstein – an executive specializing in travel and meetings management – to streamline travel policy, improve corporate collaboration across each business unit and country, and facilitate better company communication using Web 2.0 technology. Lichtenstein, well-practised in the arts of corporate reinvention, set about instigating swift travel transformations – including mandating use of non-refundable airline tickets; revising Cisco's preferred air, car and hotel partners; and encouraging use of Cisco-model virtual realities as an alternative to physical travel, especially web-conferencing. Another of her early achievements was to establish a Board which deliberated on an agreed framework for transforming travel within Cisco, and which included a new "reporting dashboard" to Cisco senior managers.

But perhaps the most significant reinvention unleashed by Lichtenstein was removing the opposition between corporate prescription and professional practice. This involved a shifting of perceptions, away from the notion of Cisco professionals as employees, and instead, seeing them as consumers. "The key to securing user approval", comments Lichtenstein, "was to focus on transforming the customer experience" (in McNulty 2009). Travel policy changes at Cisco became, in effect, employee-generated. Responsibility for organizing, booking, managing and accounting for corporate travel shifted to Cisco staff, but now reframed as consumers of Cisco travel options. Of key importance to activating the DIY corporate traveller at Cisco was the use of social networking tools – including blogs, wikis, forums and web-conferencing. Instead of a travel system run by management, argued Lichtenstein, Cisco reinvented a system in which "everyone" could contribute to travel policy and management. As she explained this:

> When employees see their forum questions being answered, they buy into the policy. We have a 79% adoption of our policy. We have a 75% online booking adoption globally – in a program that includes countries where adoption is typically low, like Russia, China and Qatar. That's amazing, all because we talk to one another.
>
> *(in McNulty 2009)*

All of the efforts I have been outlining address reinvention: in the case of Cisco, the programming of change – of endless transformations – into the organizational model. These might have been efforts to reinvent the broad-ranging strategies of the company, through the collaborative work of executives on Boards and Councils. Or it might have involved efforts to reinvent the product groups Cisco focuses on, as the company in recent years has shifted into new lines of business, such as smart cameras and online health care. And, as we have seen, there have also been extensive efforts to reinvent a new-style organizational platform – such that things are made to happen within Cisco through the drive for reinvention exhibited by company staff, as evidenced by the redesign of Cisco's global corporate travel. In sum Cisco, under Chambers, became a forum for collaborative reinvention which enabled people to change – to travel in certain business directions and not others. This Cisco management style – collaboration in order to achieve better reinvention – began as an experiment which Chambers wanted to pursue, and which slowly filtered through all aspects of the company. In an age of complex, digital systems, Chambers learnt that his own professional life had grown richer, more plural; he reasoned that this should also be true of corporations and organizational life. The issue, therefore, was how to help stop organizations from undue repetition – from repeating particular professional inclinations or company preoccupations. "The hardest thing you do as leader", said Chambers "is to change something that is working well. And yet I believe that companies and leaders who do not change will get left behind. And so I had to move from command-and-control leadership to collaborative management". The radical version of this idea, pushed by Chambers, is to change not only company plans that appeared to be faltering, but also the plans and projects which worked well enough in the past. Corporate transformation, in other words, if it works, is about facilitating space for people to recognize the inescapability of reinvention – of reinvented projects.

The exact spread and depth of the power of the reinvention platform at the level of corporations and organizational life is especially difficult to assess. Cisco, as an American multinational corporation specializing in communications technology and networking services, reflects trends in the new economy, and is thus not necessarily reflective of organizational change in other sectors of the economy – although the new economy does undeniably exert a profound influence on our culture more generally. But corporate reinvention is exceedingly difficult to assess for another reason too. That is, that reinvention at the organizational level tends to become self-propelling, as each new wave of corporate reinvention is met with calls for deeper and more comprehensive revision of received practices, beliefs and assumptions than was required previously. At Cisco, this has more recently translated as a major redesign of the company's reorganized management structure of Boards and Councils. In brief, Cisco decided in 2011 to downsize the number of Councils from nine to three, and to switch focus from broad-ranging company strategies to products and services. Such a revision of the corporate arts of reorganization is hardly surprising from a company such as Cisco: this is the idiom of a multinational effortlessly at home in the world of reinvention. But it may, of course, be worth asking why what made sense in corporate terms quite recently, no longer makes so much sense now. What exactly has changed? A useful clue comes from Chambers: "companies and leaders who do not change will get left behind". Business as usual demands change, which in turns begets further change – and on and on, in a kind of infinite regress. In a curious paradox, what makes reinvention so engrossing or absorbing is its experimental cast, and yet it is precisely the open-ended nature of social experiments that means there is no final point of arrival. In other words, the project of corporate reinvention – something that leaders and executives decide to do – is experienced as an imperative. From this angle, the innovation unleashed by Cisco under Chambers might be said to have arisen from his widening of the whole repertoire of reinvention experiments that the company had been prepared to undergo.

What remains of vital significance to the entire redrafting of the Cisco project under the leadership of Chambers is speed. Speed refers of course to the capacity to undertake activities fast, and in the case of Cisco's corporate reinvention what has been witnessed is the unleashing of a breakneck speed. Speed, under Chambers's reinvention of Cisco, has been used not only to create new operations but to destroy others as well. From this angle, the underscoring of speed becomes a central driver in the reorganization of the corporation's capacity for swiftness and multiplicity rather than specialization or depth. Hence, Cisco's 30 market adjacencies. But there is another sense, too, in which speed becomes interwoven with reinvention in the corporate field. Chambers's stress on speed as contributing to a positive form of co-operation speaks to the new reinvention culture of companies and corporations. It is not just a matter of doing things faster, but understanding that the reinvention of the corporation is a complex collaborative project of speed. In this conception, speed is lifted up a gear, significantly altering people's pace of life. John Tomlinson, in *The Culture of Speed*, writes of speed reconstituted as immediacy. The condition of immediacy is speed pressed to its limits. For Chambers, indeed, this is a description of Cisco Systems – with its transnational operations, virtual collaborations, and global networks, coalitions and teams.

Reinventing innovation: open, experimental, fast

So corporate reinvention has its foundation in speed – but the culture of immediacy, paradoxically, strikes at the core of all foundations. The condition and consequence of immediacy – in a 24/7 corporate world of communication technologies and virtual networks – is that of an ever-expanding diffusion, multiplicity and transformation of business possibilities. In a world of endless downsizings, electronic offshorings, short-term contracts, just-in-time deliveries and multiple careers, speed is the mantra by which the economic system legitimates itself. The speed with which new connections, coalitions and networks can be accessed is precisely the speed at which new profit-maximizing ventures can be launched. And, as we will see in the next chapter, this is one way in which reinvention, speed and global networks come to be intricately intertwined.

If speed is an essential element of reinvention society, it is among other things because it accelerates pathways for human co-operation. The culture of immediacy underpins some kind of common reinvention framework in which connection, co-operation and collaboration are advanced. Interestingly the European Internet Foundation, a group of progressive MEPs (Members of the European Parliament), recently identified "mass collaboration" as the most significant driver in business innovation. The Foundation sees transnational, open collaboration as the single most dominant paradigm in organizational innovation over the coming decades. Open, creative, transnational innovations of the kind underscored by the Foundation involve various private organizations and institutions, NGOs (nongovernmental organizations), global research networks and state agencies working together to develop business model innovation in ways unattainable by single companies. Such open innovation is prominent in some sectors of the new economy, especially industry technology. One recent Canadian example captures well the dynamics of such open innovation. The Institute for Citizen-Centred Services of Canada has brought together a range of institutional actors via creative public-private partnerships, digital technology start-ups, business process re-engineering and service-level outsourcing. The result, according to Martin Curley, Chair of the European Union Open Innovation and Strategy Polity Group, has been improved citizen services at considerably lower costs.

Is the European Internet Foundation's "open innovation" business model just pie in the sky? Maybe. Certainly success in product, service and technology innovation is difficult enough, even when economic conditions are favourable. But an open innovation business model is not only about product or service innovation. It is also, and fundamentally, about innovation at the level of organizational structure. Innovation in this sense is really about organizational reinvention, which in turn can generate added value for the firm, company or corporation which develops the innovation. Companies such as Cisco Systems and Apple are sublime innovators in this connection.

Advocates of transnational forms of open innovation – such as Curley – are surely right to emphasize the creative dynamism arising from such mass collaboration. But what is really at stake here, I think, is the explicit recognition that innovation hinges on *experiments*: on bringing together actors, groups, advisors, researchers and others – trying things out and trying things on, without any certainty of outcome. The experimental thrust of much reinvention is a dislocating, shattering, open-ended force which breaks the cast of traditional organizational practices and remakes human subjects in its wake. The call to experiment is in itself a disruptive demand, one which calls on women and men to go beyond established ways of doing things and known ways of living lives.

In addition to the experimental nature of genuine innovation, there also lie mobilities – physical, communicative, virtual and imaginative. In our high-tech, highly globalized world, "togetherness" and "collaboration" are in fact by-words for mobility. This concerns the advancement of "life on the move" undertaken by contemporary women and men, which adds up to the kind of existence that John Urry and I have elsewhere termed "mobile lives". These are lives embedded in a range of complex, dense networks – organizational, communicational, virtual. Trading ideas in and across such networks is where much "innovation action" is to be found in these early days of the twenty-first century. What emerges here, to repeat, is a chance or prospect for innovation. Beyond the realms of organized ways of doing things, innovation is open, plural and embedded in multidimensional transnational networks. It is, above all, radically experimental and fast. Yet the thrills and spills of corporate reinvention depend crucially upon access to such networks. What matters especially is access to information – its production, circulation, transmission – and of knowing how to move in and across a field of expanding networks. This raises the thorny question of inclusions and exclusions from networks and the whole emergence of networks of reinvention – which is the topic of the next chapter.

5

NETWORKS OF REINVENTION

What kind of fresh reinvention does today's new era demand? For Generation Y, those born between 1979 and 1990, reinvention belongs to a world of 24/7 multi-media and social networking sites, technological multi-tasking and informational politics. Generation Y, also known as the Internet Generation, iGeneration or MyPod Generation, regard pre-packaged reinvention scripts, products and services sceptically; Gen Y's prefer the creation of their own reinvention profiles, which are fashioned as "posted" profiles, status updates, blogs or video uploads on Twitter, MySpace or YouTube. Today, you are what you post online. In this sense, reinvention becomes digital. Reinvention, among other things, comes to mean the home page, profiles, connections, links and tags – in short, communications media and Web 2.0. This is, in effect, reinvention recast as Facebook.

As it happens, the phenomenon of Facebook is worth briefly considering in connection with the recasting of reinvention – if only because more than 80 per cent of upscale Generation Y's use Facebook daily. In 2012, there were approximately 800 million users of Facebook worldwide, a figure that has been estimated to exceed 1 billion people in the near future. As a company that began life as a social network for Harvard University students only, the growth of Facebook has been exponential. Indeed, some analysts have valued Facebook in excess of $US100 billion. Whilst the bulk of Facebook's revenue derives from advertisements positioned near user's news feeds, one of the central features that this social network site facilitates is *digital reinvention*. Many users engage with Facebook as a single platform on which to post personal details, status updates, as well as matters affecting their private and professional lives. Some see in this emergence of digital identities new possibilities for self-experimentation and self-reinvention, the opening out of a novel digital frontier, in which the ability to "post identities" through an endless engagement with distant others facilitates new forms of community and categories of friendship. On this view, Facebook both trades on and updates past ways of reinventing the self in relation to others – with the refashioning of identity through meeting "strangers" online.

Other media analysts, however, strongly disagree. Social networking sites, such as Facebook, do not so much facilitate self-reinvention through an engagement with others – though this often occurs. Rather, social networking sites expedite the articulation, transformation and reinvention of *networked individualism*. That is to say, the bright young things who log onto Facebook courtesy of their iPhone or BlackBerry are deep in trading connections and displaying networks. On this view, what is new about reinvention today is the refashioning of the News Feed, the recalibration of links and the reconstruction of networks. To reinvent in this idiom is to articulate and advertise social networks both online and offline. "Social network sites", writes Sam Han, "facilitate the visualisation of users' pre-existing, offline social networks" (2011, p. 57). In other words, in retrieving already fashioned connections and networks established offline, social network sites undertake the vital work of reinvention through transformations of the digital landscape involving the home page, news feed, tagging, upload and post. It is in this novel blending of the offline and online, as we shall see later, that Web platforms such as Facebook and Twitter recast the whole radius of reinvention.

The arts of digital reinvention

Above all, the new benefits and demands of digital reinvention have sprung up in a world for which networks have become more and more important. "Whenever we look at life", writes complexity analyst Fritjof Capra, "we look at networks" (1996: 82). The concept of networks emerged as a critique of the cultivation of connections forged between people largely through face-to-face conduct, as well as formal and informal connections between groups, organizations and institutions. Yet the notion of network in our own time has been substantially transfigured as a result of the consequences of advanced globalization. Today networks involve an array of technologies, transmissions, terminals and satellites that reflect complex reorganizations of time and space on an astonishing scale. Such transformations form what Yochai Benckler calls, in *The Wealth of Networks*, the advent of the "networked information economy" (2006:3). The idea of the global economy as networked, organized through instantaneous and simultaneous communications technology, is one that extends the powers of reinvention into a vast array of different systems, platforms and nodes. It also lies at the heart, as we shall see, of how reinvented networks interconnect and overlap with other networks of reinvention.

What is the significance of global networks to the speed and scale of reinvention? It is that networks drastically extend the scope of reinvention. Indeed, the whole terrain of reinvention is transformed as a result of the technological extensions wrought by global networks. Consider once again Facebook, specifically the posting of biographical information about users. The "profile" of a user is key, not only to the dissemination of biographical information, but also the presentation of connections of various social and professional kinds. The profile is the place where the personal and public, face-to-face connections and networked connectedness, meet. In presenting information about one's age, gender, education and workplace, as well as lifestyle choices such as leisure pursuits and hobbies, the user constructs not only a self-narrative but also a narrative of networked connections. The profile, to be sure, is a form of "self-writing" geared towards the display of chains of intermediaries, friends in common and collegial connections. Network multiplication of this kind comes about on Facebook through the functioning of a "Wall" – which permits other users to make contact, post comments or leave links. Like most social network sites, the Facebook profile is thus always transformable; a kind of "container" for where one network ends and another begins.

In this networked world, what is central to reinvention is the interconnection and overlapping of networks themselves. It is through the finding of known connections within a network, or uncovering of a colleague or friend in common through a short chain of acquaintances, that leads people to say: "it's a small world". The idea that people's distinct networks do in fact overlap was cemented in the phrase "six degrees of separation" – the notion that people are on average only six steps away, by way of connection, from any other person on the planet. As a consequence of new information technologies and the spread of global networks, however, the world has shrunk considerably further. Recent research suggests that the average number of acquaintances separating any two people in the world is not six but 4.74. The finding comes from a research experiment conducted with 721 million Facebook users, which as it happens is not an insignificant cohort given that this represents more than one-tenth of the global population. The revised, small world figure of 4.74 was calculated by computing a vast number of sample paths among Facebook users, and again powerfully underscores the intricate interconnections between networks, acquaintanceship and informational flows.

Reinventing connections and network capital

So far I have suggested in this chapter that the reinvention of lives and relationships has been profoundly modified by new communications technology – in particular, by global communication networks. The advent of Web 2.0 and now Web 3.0, specifically the array of technologies, devices and applications that facilitate global networks of interactive communication, has significantly altered the social forms and cultural formats by which identities become reinvented. If women and men enjoy posting status updates on sites like Twitter and Facebook, this is partly because social networking shapes new interactive connections and interpersonal relationships around common interests. There is nothing necessarily isolating about communication in the digital age and arguably there is a potential multiplication of reinvention practices via the endless circulations of SMS, blogs, vlogs, wikis, podcasts and the like.

At the same time, networking practices become central to redefinitions of the self, which can be either trivial or highly consequential. The spread of the Internet, digital media, wireless communication and a variety of tools of innovative software – I have argued – is intricately connected with the "shrinking" of the degrees of separation of each person from everyone else on the globe. This is known as the "small world thesis", and I have suggested that increased broadband capacity, creative open-source software and new forms of digital networking appear to be shrinking further the degree of separation of the world's population. One way of thinking about this is that global communication networks are pitching individuals from diverse sectors (cultural, social, economic) licentiously together. We are now witnessing, on the grid of digital communication, a dramatically fast rewriting of the rules, regulations and rewards of social engagement – with novel combinations of sociability, experimentation and reinvention emerging.

In one sense, the reinvention shift inaugurated through globally connected networks of information on the Internet has merely intensified already existing social practices. Consider, for example, social networks in the broadest sense. Traditionally, one of the benefits of being connected to others – on a purely instrumental level – arises from new opportunities (both personal and professional) occurring within any given network. Sociologist Mark Granovetter has spoken from this angle of the "strength of weak ties" (1983). Granovetter's research, conducted in the 1980s, revealed that more than 80 per cent of people seeking new jobs were able to exploit the assistance of others they did not know well in order to help secure a new position. In a twist of the dictum "it's not what you know, it's who you know", Granovetter argued that weak ties of acquaintanceship are fundamental to successful job searches and, by implication, to many other reinvention processes as well. Yet if we shift from the 1980s to the 2010s, something else seems to be at work – something quite new – as regards the "strength of weak ties" when embedded in digital networks. Just think, for instance, of the extent to which the Internet and digital communication technologies have extended the possible reach of weak ties – especially as regards the interconnected threads of globalization, digitization and networking.

Today, what is remarkable about the strength of weak ties is their embedding in networks of reinvention. Indeed, reinvention operates in a different sphere through communication networks and the architecture of the Internet. For one thing, the reinvention mantra is not just relayed to proximate others in a social network, but rather is posted, forwarded and tweeted on various social network sites – on Twitter, Tumblr, Facebook,

LinkedIn and YouTube. Another change in spreading word of one's impulse to reinvent stems from the increased communicative capacity through wireless networks. Today, thanks to enhanced computer graphics and interface, people upload photo-sharing and video content via media editing applications such as Apple's iPhoto. Photo uploads and video streaming, in particular, are especially favoured forms of media production and consumption by younger generations worldwide, and again act as a reminder of the broadened delivery platform for many digital products of reinvention.

All this has proven something of a windfall for many companies and organizations now able to mine social networking sites for potential job hires. Certainly a good deal of job recruitment occurs today through employers tapping into their employees' social networks. What we are dealing with here concerns organizations able to exploit the latest advances in technology – for example, using software to search the profiles of professionals on LinkedIn – but not cut loose from all relationship to organizational knowledge or local context; and this is pretty much why technological recruiting tools are used in tandem with personal referral processes from employees. The act of employers tapping into the contact lists of their employees' social network lists depends, of course, on a personal referral process – usually negotiated through offering bonuses to those employees who assist in the task of job recruitment. Also transformative of the landscape of professional life today are those businesses that pay for recruitment services from companies like Jobvite or Appiro, which track potential employees via social networking email invitations as well as referral networks and referral bonuses. Again, the social networking site is the place where employer and employee, transformation and reinvention, come together.

The image of the new economy as a web, or a network of networks (for example, the Internet) consisting of delicately interlaced distant connections, also has professional consequences for individuals. To begin with, it is not just companies and businesses that become proactive in exploiting social networking sites for improved ways of doing things but also professionals, who increasingly are encouraged to view social media as an exercise in personal branding. This, then, appears as an argument for the networked leveraging of professional profiles. The very interwovenness of networked connections, which means that reinvention comes to equate to personal branding online, is underscored by American personal branding guru Dan Schawbel (2011) in the following five rules for reinvention via social media.

1. Leverage Your Social Graph.
2. Use Augmented Reality and Job Search Apps.
3. Build Your Online Influence.
4. Use Multimedia Instead of a Paper Résumé.
5. Turn Yourself in an Advertisement.

In Schawbel's relentless drone of the can-do mantra, there is of course a large dose of voluntarism. Reinvention, for Schawbel, is a human subject without external constraint and without a final destination. As there is no centre to a network, no focal point which would allow the individual to achieve an enduring reinvention of self, the only viable course of action is to spread your reinvention message along as many communications, networks and nodes as possible. Reinvention is thus the stuff of endlessly proliferating links, unplanned connections and unpredictable movement. Indeed, movement is in many ways the core of this doctrine, since the quick response and fast transformations are essential to navigating the more or less instantaneous and simultaneous communications that underpin networks of reinvention.

In a world of the Internet, digital media, wireless communication, innovative open-source software, blogs, vlogs and wikis, the malleability of reinvention unfolds against the backdrop of "life on the move". In a previous book, *Mobile Lives*

(2010), John Urry and I developed the argument that the mobility acceleration underpinning people's lives today, not only physical travel but also communicative and virtual mobility, plays a central role in the recasting of reinvention in terms of flexibility, plasticity, adaptability and instant transformation. From laptops and mobile phones to teleworking, from blogging to videoconferencing, many lives in the rich North today are being reinvented as a result of hugely complex mobility systems. To grasp the reinvention of life on the move, Urry and I invoked the term "network capital", from which the resources for networking emerge, along with a strenuously self-affirmative framing of connectedness in order to participate within networks of reinvention. As we developed the argument (2010:10–11), there are eight core elements of network capital:

1. an array of appropriate documents, visas, money, qualifications that enable safe movement of one's body from one place, city, country to another
2. others (workmates, friends and family members) at-a-distance that offer invitations, hospitality and meetings so that places and networks are maintained through intermittent visits and communications
3. movement capacities in relationship to the environment: to walk distances within different environments, to be able to see and board different means of mobility, to be able to carry or move baggage, to have readable timetabled information, to be able to access computerized information, to arrange and re-arrange connections and meetings, the ability, competence and interest to use mobile phones, text messaging, email, the internet, Skype, etc.
4. location free information and contact points: fixed or moving sites where information and communications can arrive, be stored and retrieved, including real/electronic diaries, address books, answerphone, secretary, office, answering service, email, web sites, mobile phones

5. communication devices: to make and remake arrangements especially on the move and in conjunction with others who may also be on the move
6. appropriate, safe and secure meeting places: both en route and at the destination(s) including office, club space, hotel, home, public spaces, street corner, café, interspaces, that ensure that the body is not exposed to physical or emotional violence
7. access to car, road space, fuel, lifts, aircraft, trains, ships, taxis, buses, trams, minibuses, email account, internet, telephone and so on
8. time and other resources to manage and coordinate 1–7, especially when there is a system failure, as will intermittently happen.

Network capital is less an individualistic notion than a communications-driven and information-based idea. People who enjoy high levels of network capital experience high levels of geographical mobility, extensive institutional contacts, and are "at home" in, and moving across, many diverse settings. What especially matters is information – its production, transmission, circulation and, above all, sharing. To have high network capital is to join a field of ever-expanding networks, the core of a "mobile life".

New burdens: the limits of networked reinvention

The first age of the Internet reached its highpoint in the closing years of the twentieth century. This era of major technological innovation, and its associated flourishing of various global networks, is doubtless complex and contradictory. Yet there are clear affinities between the arrival of the Internet age and the emergence of new forms of identity transformation and cultural reinvention at large. The promise of the period, at least as far as reinvention goes, was well captured by American sociologist Sherry Turkle in her book *Life On The Screen* (1995). By focusing on first-generation Internet relay chat rooms and text-based virtual reality sites, Turkle drew attention to the pos-sibilities of digital media to segment our identities and reinvent our lives. A specific concern of Turkle's book was the spread of "netsex", in particular, the impact of cybersex upon rein-ventions of the self, undertaken through experiments with pseudonyms and other linguistic markers of identity. According to Turkle's analysis, cybersex is intrinsically transformable and transforming. At the click of a mouse, individuals can rein-vent themselves, switching effortlessly from flirtation to cross-dressing, from sadomasochism to fetishism. Turkle writes, for example, of the emotional dilemmas of a young man who dis-covers that his girlfriend habitually casts herself as a man online and engages in cybersex with female characters in chat rooms. Reinvention is written in to the very virtual dynamics of cyber-sex according to Turkle, akin to a lifting of the playful aesthetics of postmodernism to the second power.

The arrival of the 2000s and emergence of Web 2.0, however, brought with it no equivalent expectation of the powers of digital reinvention. As social networking sites deepened and diversified their operations, the goal of controlling our digital identities – their segmentations, proliferations and reinventions – shattered. Instead, the harsh reality of virtual life unfolded: the reinvention of digital identities is at once public and permanent, lodged or posted "forever", and retrievable at the click of a mouse. On this view, the Web equals the death of forgetting. In terms of the perils of the digital age, there is thus something daunting about the permanent memory bank of the Internet. A world in which everything is recorded, then, is our new nor-mative condition – where every status update, online photo, Twitter post, blog entry and video upload can be retrieved in an instant. What initially promised to be a self-expanding, attrac-tively ambitious medium for reinvention is thus revealed instead as limiting the possible range of public and private identities. If the Internet never forgets, this significantly recasts the capacity of everyone from political leaders and celebrities to citizens to control what kind of information about the self is accessed, retrieved and re-posted in various communicative contexts. Rather than open-ended reinvention, we find a Web of regret – in which past moments of forgivable weakness or salacious scandal are forever present to the world.

There is perhaps something rather too menacing in this reckoning of the burden of digital lifestyles. That said there are more and more sectors of life in which the meshing of online and offline identities carries profound new social consequences. A survey conducted by Microsoft in 2012, for example, revealed that over 75 per cent of human resource professionals in the United States conduct online research about job candidates – checking everything from personal blogs to social networking sites to online-gaming activities. If the digital discoveries relating to a job candidate's online narrative are too flirtatiously disabling, or incongruously at odds with the presentational demands of the profession, then swift rejection is likely to follow. Some detective work surrounding a job candidate's prior professional experience or personal dispositions has always been part of the brief of recruiters and human resource professionals. In the brave new world of third-party tracking of Web surfing, however, the online trace of previous self-presentations and self-reinventions takes on rather different implications for the conduct of offline identities.

There are many indicators that "private lives" are in the process of being privatized by the new communications environment. In 2011, Facebook announced – in one privacy-killing move – that parts of the digital profiles of its users that were previously tagged private (including details of relationship status and family relations) would become public on the site. This unleashed a sea of criticism, and Facebook CEO Mark Zuckerberg appeared throughout various media with reassurances about new privacy settings. But still there are other creditable reasons for asserting an emergent wholesale liquidation of the private sphere in our digital age. For one thing, the

US Library of Congress announced – also in 2011 – that it will acquire and permanently store the complete archive of public Twitter posts since 2006. This archive, to be sure, is of public posts; yet it is difficult not to intuit significant changes in the relations between the public and private spheres occurring. Privacy in such conditions becomes perhaps more a matter of posts, p2p networks and protocols of communication.

The arguments about privacy in the digital age will doubtless continue, not least because advances in technological innovation are unfolding at a giddying pace, thus outstripping our inherited categories for dividing life into sectors of the personal and the public. But what is noted here are the emergent counter-strategies – some resistant, others transformative – which seek to bring the concern over privacy to contemporary global society. Underscoring the global reach of a Web that never forgets, the European Union recently financed a campaign titled "Think B4 U post!" Around the globe, activists and artists are working on projects to "reinvent forgetting on the Internet", highlighting ingenious ways to make data disappear. Yet not all such counter-strategies are staged in the name of the public good, or of rights. A range of commercial enterprises, for example, have muscled in on various forms of Internet reputation bankruptcy, providing services to recover, repair and even delete negative information about individuals and organizations. Reputation-Defender is one such enterprise, reportedly with customers in over one hundred countries, monitoring and cleaning up the "soiled" online identities of its customers.

Reinvention and co-creation

For many people, Starbucks has become synonymous with "coffee culture". Whether you like or dislike Starbucks coffee, it is clear that the company has brought about a reinvention of coffee culture through a seemingly limitless multiplication and development of its services and products. Like many transnational companies, this it has done through digital marketing strategies – especially social media. Starbucks is one of the most popular global brands on Facebook, with over 10 million followers, and it has also regularly deployed "Promoted Tweets" on Twitter. To advertise the idea of Starbucks as a remouldable, flexible brand through social media has been a swift solution to the challenges of corporate reinvention. But in addition, Starbucks has also engaged with social media so that customers can play a role in transforming its products and services. The establishing of the "My Starbucks Idea" site is one example, where consumers devised ways of improving the whole Starbucks experience. From ideas concerning electronic loyalty rewards and Starbucks apps for the iPhone, to innovations, such as "Free Pastry Day" (which drove over a million extra customers to purchase coffee to claim a free pastry), consumers have taken on a central role in helping reinvent the Starbucks brand. With the launch of new social media and its associated narrative of greater consumer participation, we have now entered the terrain of *co-creation*. The term co-creation refers in this context to the phenomenon of companies and organizations working with their customers – tapping into their creative energies – in order to better refashion products, services and experiences. Co-creation became a buzz-word in the reinvention lexicon in the early 2000s, and the results have often enjoyed global reach. In the case of Starbucks, for example, the launch of the highly successful Frappuccino was a result of customer-made co-creation.

We tend to think of creativity as pertaining to the self, or as something that can occur in organizations as a result of individuals working together. Only more recently has the idea of creativity as a distributed platform arisen, in part, as a result of the spread of digital culture. The links between creativity and innovation, or in today's idiom co-creation and reinvention, are certainly complex and contradictory, but interesting lines of development are discernible. If co-creation is integral to reinvention, it is equally central to the innovations of consumer society. One area in which this Reinvention Reformation plays out with a vengeance today is the increasing involvement of consumers in corporate advertising. From L'Oreal's "You Make The Commercial" to McDonald's "Global Casting" advertising campaigns, consumers have been directly drawn into the process by which products and services are designed, developed and disseminated. This is, no doubt, partly a matter of corporations realizing the loyalty benefits of involving customers in their operations, but also perhaps a question of pressing the creative skills of consumers into the design of goods, services and experiences which they desire and will consume.

Co-creation then has been among other things a way of keeping reinvention fresh, an extension of the whole reinvention mantra in contemporary times. Increasingly, though, co-creation signals not only customer-made reinvention through advertising but also the reinvention of product and service development by consumers. In one sense, the point is not simply to outsource marketing to loyal customers, but to secure and advance such brand loyalty through the consumer's ideas for reinvention. In a world of do-it-yourself, customization and privatization, it is perhaps easy to miss the significance of this deepening of the reinvention idiom. The phrase "customer reinvention" really comes into its own with consumer-made product and service development, and there has been no shortage of transnational companies and businesses championing customer-made reinvention in the 2000s. Nokia's "Concept Lounge" is a good example, in which consumers were invited to share ideas online, and in effect take on the brief of designing the next Nokia mobile device. Such outsourcing of reinvention to customer-made has multiplied endlessly. From Nespresso's "Design Contest" (resulting in the Nespresso InCar coffee machine) to Peugeot's "Concours Design" (which led to the Moovie, a two-seater electric concept car), companies have outsourced product innovation and design to consumers in search of the Next Big Thing.

6

THE REINVENTION OF PLACES

The idea of reinvention, while glamorous, is not necessarily the most racy these days. What is racy instead is *mega*-reinvention. It is one thing to reinvent a lifestyle or identity, but to reinvent a whole city is undeniably to shift things up a gear. Mega-reinvention is today the clarion call of transnational corporations and speculative global investment, with its unleashing of the cult of architectural monumentality, fortresses of extravagance and infinite consumption excess. Mega-malls, mega-resorts, mega-hotels, mega-airports, mega-metropolises: today's reinvention of places is offered up in the name of gigantism, in a culture obsessed with having the biggest, best, largest, shiniest and newest of everything. This shifting of the cultural terrain from reinvention to mega-reinvention is especially ironic. In an historic unleashing of the technological powers of advanced globalization, mega-reinvention represents not only a new global narrative of capitalism but also an inexhaustible narcissism, one which rides roughshod over nature. Nothing appears to stand in the way of the cultural desire for mega-reinvention and its unflagging energy which, in an era of global warming and climate change, is suggestive of hubris on the grandest of scales.

Even so, mega-reinvention is everywhere and has helped to advance the dynamism of the global electronic economy in dramatic ways. Consider, for example, the European destination city of leisure, Gran Scala, a €17 billion entertainment project that comprises 32 casinos, 232 restaurants, 70 hotels, five theme parks, a race track and a bullring. Located in the Spanish desert where water and oil are scarce, Gran Scala is symptomatic of present-day reinvention excess: an ambitionless, all-consuming place of transformation which is impervious to any ecological reality. Other mega-paradises of reinvention are also worth noting. In Singapore, Marina Bay Sands, which opened in 2010, is the world's most expensive casino resort, boasting a 2561 room hotel, a 1,300,000 ft² convention centre, a mega-mall, a museum, two floating Crystal Pavilions and an ice skating rink. In the USA, American Dream Meadowlands, scheduled to open in 2013, is the second largest combined shopping, entertainment and sports complex in the country, and its five storey structure consists of, among others, a skidome, an indoor ice rink, a waterpark, a theme park and a skydiving simulator.

In this chapter, I shall turn to consider this broadening of the cultural logics of reinvention to that of places and spaces. Drawing on a wide range of studies, and using contemporary illustrations from popular culture and consumerism, I shall argue that the rise of the reinvention of places is inextricably intertwined with consumption excess.

Experimental reinvention: developing Dubai

If the reinvention and redesign of cities of consumption excess is indicative of the cultural logics of capitalist globalization, the prime example of it in contemporary times is Dubai. Monumental architecture, mega-shopping malls for excessive consumption, lavish hotels, blockbuster sports and entertainment events, tax-free zones, spectacular tourist attractions and theme parks: Dubai is a city of stunning opulence, glitzy glamour and conspicuous consumption. Raising the Bling of Las Vegas to the second power, Dubai is an uncanny mixture of desire and desperation – or, in the language of reinvention society, of addiction and fear. Redeveloped endlessly since the 1970s to become the world's largest building site, Dubai is a city of obscene enjoyment, as well as a site of extreme exploitation and devastating destruction. We shall be looking at the emotional and environmental costs of Dubai's meteoric reinvention a little later, but to begin with it is necessary to briefly chart the city's spectacular interweaving of excessive consumerism and themed tourism.

Dubai's glass-and-steel skyline, which rises out of the desert beside the Persian Gulf, tells the dramatic story of rapid reinvention – at once intensive and extensive. This was a city that, during the 1950s when a part of the British protectorate, did not have any international hotels. Today, it is littered with lavish hotels – the tallest, biggest and newest on the planet. The cultural logic of reinvention proposed a master idea for Dubai, a city that became fast reconciled to technology, mass tourism and consumer culture, that would be globalized, hi-tech, cosmopolitan and commercialized. Consider, for example, some of the following developments just in respect of hotels alone:

- The world's first 7-star hotel, the Burj Al Arab, was built in 1999 and consists of 321 metres of rocket-ship inspired architecture, with suites including rain showers and Jacuzzis, a 24/7 butler service and a Rolls-Royce fleet.
- The Atlantis Hotel in Dubai offers ostentatious glamour and consumer excess, with suites that cost $US35,000 per night, which includes a direct view into a one-million-litre aquarium stocked with 14,000 fish.
- The world's largest planned hotel, the Asia-Asia, is awaiting construction and is expected to offer 6,500 rooms. The project

is part of a larger construction run by Bawadi, which is developing 60,000 themed hotel rooms in Dubai.

The sheer excess of these developments – in terms of scale and super-size – is emblematic of the reinvention ethos which has gripped Dubai. It is a city of, and for, global elites, celebrities and the super-rich. But thanks to the global media attention Dubai has generated as a place of excess, it also functions as an aspirational city. Dubai is a kind of dream-world that people hanker for and after, in the hope that just some of the frantic reinvention logic of the city might rub off on them. The dramatic escalation in passenger numbers flying to holiday, shop and do business in Dubai is indicative of this. In 2000, 3.4 million tourists entered Dubai; by 2007, this figure had soared to 6.4 million. Such a boost in travel can in part be attributed to the presence of internationally renowned hotel chains – such as Hyatt, Hilton, Sheraton and Shangri-La – which set up flagship hotels in the city and are now responsible for two-thirds of the city's travel revenue.

To convert a whole travel experience into consumption excess is a powerful way of reinventing a city as a specialized place with particular services, and such a spectacular synthesis of tourism and consumerism indeed defines Dubai. The present-day reinvention of the Arabian metropolis is one that, among other things, encompasses wall-to-wall shopping. The design and construction of mega-malls of consumption excess sprawl across Dubai – audaciously super-sized, highly commercialized and with many simulated environments. Dubai's cathedrals of consumption – including the Dubai Mall, the Mall of The Emirates, IBN Butunna Mall and Reef Mall – entice shopaholics the world over, with their lavish mix of top-end designer stores and indulgent facilities, ranging from aquariums to indoor ski slopes. Similarly, eye-popping themed environments are also part of the city's reinvention mix. Simulated environments are one essential ingredient of contemporary cultures of consumption, and Dubai's imitation of various global iconic structures is arguably equal to, if not more "real" than, the original from which they are copied. Consider, for example, the Dubai Fountain – a copy of Las Vegas's Bellagio's fountain, but on a grander scale. Or the massive simulacra for play of Dubailand, a planned theme park to be twice the size of Disney World – and scheduled to include a Universal Studios, London Eye-inspired wheel and underwater hotel.

Dubai's reinvention as a destination for tourist luxury and excess has also bred its correlative vices of gambling, alcohol, drugs and prostitution. This glistening Arabian metropolis is it once a realm of excess and addiction. Those living "lives of addiction" are drawn to exceptional and playful attractors, offered *ad infinitum* throughout Dubai, in order to unlock the emotional highs of excess – with people reinventing their identities through compulsive dependencies of infinite consumption, the sex industry or gambling. There are, to be sure, excessively exploitative kinds of dispossession too, such as the hundreds of thousands of migrant contract labourers travelling from countries such as India and Pakistan, seduced by the lure of construction jobs in Dubai. The deprivations of Dubai's hard-pressed migrant workers, estimated at up to 90 per cent of the city's labouring workforce, has been extensively documented. From corrosive corruption to slave-like exploitation, migrant workers are sucked inexorably into a realm of reinvention in which their identities are all but fully cancelled out. Most migrant labourers have their passports confiscated upon entry into Dubai. In doing so, these men are rendered unidentifiable and hence as objects of excessive exploitation. Much of the time, at least, migrant contract workers have been expected to work up to 18 hour days, and often have failed to receive remuneration. This is the "dark side" of the Dubai that thrives on transgressing boundaries. In its sublime reinvention and extravagant consumerism, Dubai conceals the most obnoxious dispossession of lives, in which migrants and the working poor suffer abominable repression and humiliation.

It is no surprise, also, that the rapid reinvention of Dubai has been purchased at severe environmental costs. The reinvention of Dubai from desert to megatropolis has been underpinned by the vast use of oil to transport workers and tourists, an unsustainable use of water and energy, along with a dissolute use of raw materials for massive construction and building projects. In all of this, nature and the environment has been the enemy, and its opposite has been speculative property development. Domination over nature has been the central motif for the refashioning of Dubai as one of the highest carbon and water-depleting societies on the planet. In the conflict between nature and culture, or environment and reinvention, the answer for Dubai came in the form of desalination plants. To desalinate sea water seemed the perfect solution to an environment that offered no usable fresh water, no surface water and one of the lowest rainfalls in the world. There was, however, a lethal flipside. Desalination plants have served as the foundation for Dubai's reinvention, but at a cost higher than the production of petrol. The obsession with conspicuous consumption in Dubai has resulted in a larger carbon footprint to the city per capita than that of the United States, substantially due to carbon dioxide emissions from desalination plants.

Terminal reinvention: airports and the aerotropolis

Travel, it is said, broadens the mind. Travel encourages people to desire and fantasize, and arguably nowhere more so than when it comes to airports and the lure of international journeys. In the last chapter I argued that people, in these early decades of the twenty-first century, are "on the move" as never before. Travel and tourism, for example, make up the largest industry in the world, generating in excess of $US7.5 trillion annually. Air travel has especially profited from this trend. As travel has become increasingly global, facilitated by the rise of transnational companies and budget airlines, the aviation industry has become big business. For example, 2011 witnessed a global total of some 2.75 billion airline passengers, with air travel undertaken for work-related purposes (largely by "frequent flyer" business travellers) the most prominent. This is reflective of what John Urry and I have elsewhere called the rise of "mobile lives".

Airports play a special role in this facilitation of mobile lives, and there is considerable evidence which indicates that hyper-aeromobilities are advancing the culture of reinvention to a dramatic new level. One important clue concerning social transformations arising from airports comes from artists and writers, who have been amongst the most well-trained eyes in scrutinizing the powers of reinvention. Andy Warhol captured well that airspaces are full-blooded worlds within worlds when he spoke of "the airport atmosphere". Airports, as described by Warhol (1976:145):

> have my favourite kind of food service, my favourite kind of bathrooms, my favourite peppermint Life Savers, my favourite kinds of entertainment, my favourite loudspeaker address systems, my favourite conveyer belts, my favourite graphics and colors, the best security checks, the best views, the best perfume shops, the best employees, and the best optimism.

Airports, for Warhol, involve not only a state of mind but a disposition – which means a kind of reinvention of self appropriate to "the airport atmosphere". This is a reinvention of self geared to the timeless and placeless atmosphere of the airport itself. But airports and reinvention cross and tangle in other ways too. J.G. Ballard sees airports, for example, as "the ramblas and agoras of the future city, time-free zones where all the clocks of the world are displayed, an atlas of arrivals and destinations forever updating itself, where briefly we become true world citizens" (quoted in Urry 2007, p. 151).

Ballard puts the point well, at least as far as airports functioning as emblematic of the future (and the future city) is concerned. In the past, the core business of airports – which usually arose out of military facilities and were planned and operated by national-state public bodies – concerned aeronautical infrastructure and services. But the design of airports primarily as transport hubs – as organizing structures for the arrival and departure of passengers, cargo and aircraft – has undergone significant change in the 2000s. Today, airports are increasingly broader and more capacious in scope. The contemporary airport is one reinvented as a place or locale for core aeronautical activities certainly, but also – and this is now fundamental – for non-aeronautical commercial activities, services and facilities. In a globalized world of private corporation airports (such as Heathrow in the UK) or private-public partnership airports (such as Dusseldorf in Germany), these new operational structures mix together numerous forms of travel, transport, consumerism, entertainment, business events and services, recreation facilities, and cultural attractions. As commercialized global transport hubs, airports today feature, amongst others, speciality retail, designer boutiques, duty free shops, "frequent flyer" clubs, business office complexes, convention centres, leisure facilities, hotel accommodation, and health and child care facilities.

It is perhaps hardly surprising that, in an era of advanced globalization and new communication technologies, airports are being redefined, rebranded and reinvented. Yet the compass of the reinvention of airports is staggering. It is not simply that all major airports are now continually upgrading and expanding their terminals in order to cope with the huge volume of passengers shifting through global airspace. It is also the sheer scale of the massive sprawl of new airports, of their monumental terminals of steel and glass, their skyscraper structures, their design by celebrity architects and their huge capital investments. Consider, for example, that oasis of indulgence known as Terminal 3 at the Dubai International Airport. At one stage the largest building in the world (measuring some 12.76 million square feet), Dubai International Airport's Terminal 3 is the world's largest air terminal. It consists of 97 escalators, 82 moving walkways, 157 elevators, 180 check-in counters and 2,600 parking spaces. Designed to accommodate Dubai's flagship airline Emirates's fleet of A380s, Terminal 3 is an 86,000 square-foot cathedral of consumption, in which travellers can engage in shopping around the clock. As a global transportation hub linking Dubai to economies such as Europe, the US, China and India, Terminal 3 is an airport at once commercialized, crowded, challenging and cosmopolitan.

The reinvention of airports in the image of mega-shopping malls is probably the most obvious impact arising from the spread of globalization and its culture of rampant consumerism. Globalization, however, is pushing this reinvention of the form, function and financing of airports still one step further. The more globalization intensifies the movement and mobility of people, the more airports are reshaped and redesigned to mix commerce, events and experiences. Let us briefly note just some illustrative examples in this connection. Singapore's Changi Airport offers passengers a range of innovative services, including a swimming pool, saunas and movie theatres. Beijing Capital International Airport has an extensive array of free passenger services, such as art troupe performances including singers, dancers and magicians. Amsterdam Schiphol Airport has its own Dutch Master's gallery run by the world-famous Rijksmuseum. Las Vegas McCarran Airport also operates a 24/7 museum – the Howard W. Cannon Aviation Museum. Stockholm Arlanda Airport possesses a chapel, which conducts hundreds of weddings annually. Munich Airport offers The AirportClinic M – a "full concept service", state-of-the-art medical hospital covering everything from orthopaedics to cosmetic plastic surgery. And South Korea's Incheon International Airport boasts not only an entire "golf town" (complete with 330 yard driving range and 18-hole putting course), but also what it enticingly labels

"Ice Forest" – a skating rink installed with plastic artificial ice to keep passengers dry when they fall.

Such innovations are the latest form of the reinvention of airport cultures to better serve and sustain passengers in transit. Transit time is now based not just around shopping but also the accumulation and diversification of experiences and events. Transit is no longer conceived as a passive experience, in which the passenger has time to "kill". Transit now increasingly revolves around a different concept. Since our culture promotes the ideal of do-it-yourself lifestyles and reinvented identities, so too transit time is more and more bound up with the accumulation of novel experiences, the self-design of airport services, and the innovative interspersing of leisure and work activities. From this angle, the contemporary airport comes to mean, among other things, fashion, shopping, culture, lifestyle, marketing, advertising, business, networking and communications media. Moreover, as passengers navigate the dizzying array of airport services from gyms to conference centres to art galleries, there is unfolding a massive mixing together of very many different mobile lifestyles and identities. In this sense, global air traffic results in transit spaces that juxtapose holiday-makers, business travellers, drug traders, money launderers, artists on tour, people smugglers and many others.

Reinvention, I have been suggesting, lies at the very core of the contemporary airport and especially the form and function of airport terminals. But this is not all. Above all, there are new cultural and commercial ideas which have sprung up relating to the possibilities for "airport cities" – or what John D. Kasarda calls the "aerotropolis". The reinvention of airports along the aerotropolis business model, according to Kasarda, involves the bundling of corridor development, fast connectivity, multi-modal transport infrastructure, aviation-linked business clusters and related residential developments. In one sense, the notion of aerotropolis seeks to underscore the increasing restructuring of business operations (from hotel chains to health and fitness centres) along airport corridors. The aerotropolis model, how-ever, has also arguably arisen as airports have become key attractors for regional corporations and information-intensive firms. As Kasarda (2008:15) contends:

> Firms specialising in information and communications technology and other high-tech industries consider air accessibility especially crucial. High-tech professionals travel by air 400 percent more frequently than workers in general, giving rise to the term "nerd birds" in the US for commercial aircraft connecting "techie" capitals such as Austin, Boston, Raleigh-Durham and San Jose. Many high tech firms are locating along major airport corridors, such as those along the Washington-Dulles Airport access corridor in Northern Virginia and the expressways leading to Chicago's O'Hare International Airport. In this sense, knowledge networks and air travel networks increasingly reinforce each other.

Reinvention in-flight

If the reinvention-targeted economy of consumerism is one of excess, it is also one that has morphed into a public fetish. In a society of reinventing consumers, the market for consumer products knows no limit. Consumerism in the era of the global electronic economy is, among other things, all about the endless multiplication of sites for shopping. The cultivation of shopping, of limitless accumulation, in the fields of fashion, cosmetics, exercise, diet, health, therapy, love and relationships is essential to the workings of reinvention society and its strenu-ously self-affirmative human subjects. A piling up of sites or fields for addictive consumer activities is fundamental to the advanced capitalist world. From this angle, it is globalization itself which is seductive, extravagant, out of hand – geared to the ongoing organization of consumer markets that enable – perhaps compel – reinvention.

At the same time, popular culture in the sense of shopping has become even more expansionist. The more the logics of reinvention, operationalized through consumer culture, has unfolded across the planet, the more globalizing economic forces have been driven in search of new reinvention frontiers. Beyond our planet there is, of course, the sky – and it is precisely here that the commercial airlines have sought to create a mirror-image of the reinvention marketplace. The purchase of erotically alluring commodities from 30,000 feet is now firmly entrenched as part of the in-flight experience, as professionals and tourists fly in the skies. Like shopping at the mall, in-flight shopping pitches together the lures of desire and consumption excess. Many airlines today boast mini-duty-free shops on-board, with passengers able to engage consumer reinvention to their hearts' content through the purchase of everything from skincare products to champagne, massage lounges to computers.

Meanwhile, you can find yourself earning airline miles or frequent flyer points with purchases in-flight – all presented under the banner of meeting customers' service expectations, though this is also an offering which fits hand-in-glove with the whole culture of reinvention. Earning miles or points with shopping purchases "makes sense" in as far as this fits with the cultural logics of reinvention society. For such consumerism in the skies can be glossed, ultimately, as all about improvement, change and transformation. Shopping in-flight is revealed as part of the user-friendly and pleasurable world of reinvention, in which commodities and services purchased now will be drawn into the utopic future of continuously expanding horizons.

Life in the sky thus encompasses a new emphasis on choice and product differentiation – on packaging, marketing and design. A stress on in-flight reinvention comes pre-wrapped in ideas from the consumer industries concerning the differentiation of consumers by lifestyle, taste and culture. Note that what is most significant here is the diversification of individualized consumption times and spaces. Passengers, thanks to the communications revolution, can shop at whatever times they wish. Consider, for example, Delta Air Lines, which in 2012 announced that passengers will have free connection access to Amazon.com and Amazonwireless.com through the Delta Connect Wi-Fi portal. The growth of such service innovation in-flight allows passengers to use their laptops, tablets and smartphones to engage in endless shopping and entertainment options. This new in-flight system of flexible consumption of goods has been further expanded to encompass a diversification of services and experiences also. Airlines including Virgin Atlantic, Air France and Lufthansa have established "walled" social networks built out of their existing frequent-flier memberships. Whilst only modestly successful in the first instance, due to limitations of technology, there have since been more recent attempts by airlines to deploy social networking sites in the service of passenger reinvention practices. KLM unveiled a new programme called "Meet and Seat", which allows passengers to upload Facebook or LinkedIn profiles and to use such data to select preferred seating. Likewise, Malaysia Airlines have introduced MHBuddy, a software application allowing passengers to cross-check whether any friends or colleagues are on board the same flight, and thus recalibrate their in-flight experience. Reinvention, it transpires, is not just global but a supra-planetary force!

CONCLUSION

The reign of reinvention

I began this book by noting that reinvention societies have spread everywhere now throughout the expensive polished cities of the West. Against the backdrop of the rise of globalization and the global electronic economy, and embedded within the extraordinary consumerism of Western societies, the culture of reinvention is today ubiquitous, self-propelling, ineluctably a part of the order of social life. No one can escape the perpetual manufacture of reinvention societies – of quick-fix weight loss programmes, of personal makeovers and cosmetic surgery, of speed dating and online therapies, and of business downsizings and organizational offshorings. The call to reinvent, which is intensely extravagant and always excessive, is everywhere – the reinvention of identity and of the body, of sex and relationships, of careers and corporations, and of places and the global order.

To say that reinvention society is extravagant is to say that the cult of reinvention is, among other things, shaped from the outset by excess. The whole culture of reinvention is one which knows no limit; it is always in excess of itself. Reality, within the frame of reinvention culture, is endlessly pliable. Reinvention at its inner core is curiously self-multiplying. In the broadest sense, reinvention society is self-reproducing, diffuse, hedonistic and transgressive. Consider, for example, the perverse blending of terror and delight which feeds today's fat-phobic culture. In a 24/7 world of mass media, shaped to its core by consumerism, corporatism and celebrity culture, there is an endless dissection and scrutiny of fat (and the possible emergence of fat) bodies. From daily media scrutiny of celebrity bodies for any signs of weight gain to women and men's anxieties that their diets are making them fat, reinvention society offers an endless menu of its own market-type solutions to the risks, dangers and associated social death of obesity. Media images of impossibly thin, sleek and sexualized bodies are, of course, part and parcel of this. But the excess of reinvention culture demands more; there is a kind of lethal ecstasy acted out in many media representations of reinvention, and perhaps nowhere more obviously so than in society's current denigration, mortification and humiliation of fat bodies (see Lupton 2012). The US reality TV series, *The Biggest Loser*, is suggestive of this cross of terror and delight in the dramatization of reinvention culture. Women made to stand in skimpy bras and tiny shorts, with wobbly flesh on display and zoned, whilst the audience delights in watching the punishing exercise routines undertaken by overweight contestants at the hands of expert personal trainers: this is the format in which contestants on *The Biggest Loser* seek to reinvent their bodies, in order to pass themselves off as "average" or "normal". We are dealing here with a delight in reinvention which provokes the very terror it seeks to transcend. From this angle, reinvention society is revealed as a destructive illusion, in which women and men disavow or expel that which they cannot tolerate about their lives.

If there is illusion, there is also resilience however. Reinvention is also the stuff of proliferating options, improvised alternatives and extravagant fashions. Notwithstanding the dislocating, perverse, excessive nature of the culture of reinvention – its crass commercialism, its implacable faddism, its triumphant transformationalism, and its traumatic liquidity – we are dealing with the complex, contradictory ways in which women and men subvert traditional values, create new meanings, shape new consensual codes, and experiment with life and its possibilities. From this angle, reinvention reminds us that in confronting our existing ways of doing things, we ultimately confront ourselves in the process. Only through looking at past ways of doing things and previous forms of living our lives can we critically examine and better realize our dreams and projects. Reinvention is thus, among other things, always an engagement (however minimal) with the contours of invention. Yes, reinvention society may be shot through with the illusions of consumerism or celebrity culture, but still it holds out the promise of an engagement with the more positive currents of human creation. This is one reason why contemporary women and men are held in thrall by reinvention society; it is not a question of people having the wool pulled over their eyes, rather we are considering the narratives of reinvention people tell (themselves and others) in order to cope with and confront a world of advanced globalization.

In this final part of the book I want to explore further our desire and fear, our fascination and dread about reinvention in its various forms. And I want to do this in slightly more technical language than in other sections of the book, looking in particular at some conceptual ideas drawn from the social sciences. I want to argue that when we engage in reinvention practices, in whatever ways, we move away from inherited or traditional notions of what is considered appropriate ways of doing things, or conventional ways of living lives. Reinvention is thus, in effect, an experiment with possible versions of the self, an experiment with alternative versions of social life. From this angle, reinvention can be enabling, indeed freeing; it can however also be disabling, and even pathological.

From the age of reflexivity to reinvention

In seeking to provide a wide-ranging, accessible and entertaining introduction to the topic of reinvention – spanning therapeutic reinventions of the self to corporate redesigns of multinational enterprises – this book has set out new ideas relating to contemporary transformations of self and society. My core hypothesis is that *reinvented identity-practices, spawned in conditions of advanced globalization, increasingly come to the fore in these early years of the twenty-first century*. At the core of global economies of reinvention, we find the drive to reconstruct, recalibrate, restructure and reorganize social practices, as well as the identities of agents that perform such practices. This drive to reinvention, I have argued, has become increasingly integral to contemporary living, and often enough represents a kind of "tipping point" for a multitude of contemporary addictions, obsessions and compulsions.

What helps to found reinvention society at the institutional level also figures within us, in a kind of sedimentation lodged deeply at the level of personal life and the emotions. Indeed, it is precisely the desire to better grasp the confluence of interior and exterior changes in peoples' lives today that has led me to propose the notion of "reinvention" as a key driver in both personal and professional life. At the core of this reinvention orientation there lies a deep cultural fascination for, and institutional pressure towards, change. Today's culture of reinvention carries profound consequences for reorganizing the relations between self and society. In sociological terms, "reinvention society" cuts both externally and internally. The triumph of globalization is that it not only operates on a horizontal axis, universalizing the operations of multinational capital and new digital technologies across the globe; it operates also, and fundamentally, on a vertical axis, reorganizing identities and pressing the ethos of reinvention into its service. This is not an argument about subjective dispositions in relation to the social world, but rather a deeply sociological engagement with the constitution of the self in conditions of advanced globalization. In current social circumstances – in which personal lives are reshaped by technology-induced globalization and the transformation of capitalism – it is not the particular individuality of an individual which is most important. What is increasingly significant is how individuals *re-create* identities, the cultural forms through which people symbolize individual expression and desire, and perhaps above all the speed with which identities can be reinvented and instantly transformed. It is this stress on instant transformation – and in particular the fears and anxieties it is designed to displace or lessen – which distinguishes the theory of reinvention society from other characterizations of our age in the social sciences, as we will now see.

One of the more interesting mysteries of the current era is how people negotiate the huge explosion in choice which the global electronic economy has ushered into existence. People have no choice, we might say, but to choose. This dramatic expansion of choice is obviously evident in our extraordinary consumer culture, but also is increasingly evident in professional life and work, in relationships and family life, in travel and tourism, and in various other sectors of social life. What is most striking, and this begins as a result of the spread of choice, is that women and men must increasingly think about options, possibilities, pathways, chances and alternatives. What is also striking is that globalization makes detectives of us all: we monitor ourselves and each other, we closely observe the latest changes and trends of social life, and we navigate social possibilities in the quest for pleasure. All of this occurs in the institutional context of globalization, and its spawning of new information technologies and rampant consumerism. All of this takes place within the frame of, in the title of sociologist Anthony Giddens's book, our *Runaway World*. This is a world which, according to Giddens, is shaped to its core by reflexivity. That is to say, a world of increased self-monitoring, observation, recording, revising and reorganization.

But what, exactly, is meant by the notion of reflexivity? And how does it operate? Reflexivity, as elaborated by Giddens, is seen as a self-defining process that depends upon monitoring of, and reflection upon, psychological and social information about possible trajectories of life. Such information about self and world is not simply incidental to contemporary social life; it is actually constitutive of what people do and how they do it. "The reflexivity of modern social life", writes Giddens, "consists in the fact that social practices are constantly examined and reformed in the light of incoming information about those very practices, thus constitutively altering their character" (1990: 38).

Consider, as an example of how reflexivity operates in contemporary societies, the connections between marriage, the family and self-identity. There are few areas of social life that more directly affect the self than that of marriage and the family. Traditionally, the marriage tie was primarily structured as an economic arrangement: the husband used the marriage as a place from which to organize his activities in the public world, while the wife concentrated on children and the home. The idea of romantic love significantly weakened the power of such economic considerations, although marriage as an institution within patriarchy has undoubtedly remained intimately interwoven with economic power. Marriage of the late modern type, in Western societies at any rate, has provided an institutional context in which men and women can pursue the achievement of intimacy, respect, love, equality, autonomy and self-integrity. Notwithstanding changes in the relationship between the sexes in recent decades, the notion of romantic love remains psychologically central to the pursuit of personal and sexual fulfillment within marriage. Alongside this, marriage has been a key arena for the psychic development of the self, as this is organized through attitudes associated with childhood, adolescence and the nurturing of intimate sentiments within general social relations.

According to Giddens, individuals today actively engage with fresh opportunities and dangers that arise as a consequence of dramatic and shattering transformations affecting self-identity, sexuality and intimacy. For Giddens, divorce is undeniably a crisis for the self – involving pain, loss and mourning. Yet many people, he argues, take positive steps to work through the emotional dilemmas generated by marriage breakdown. In addition to dealing with financial issues and matters affecting how children should be brought up, separation and divorce also call into play an emotional engagement with the self. Charting territory of the past (where things went wrong, missed opportunities, etc.) and of the future (alternative possibilities, chances for self-actualization, etc.) necessarily involves experimenting with a new sense of self. This can lead to emotional growth, new understandings of self and strengthened intimacies. Against the conservative critique of irredeemable breakdown, Giddens sees an opening out of the self to constructive renewal. Remarriage and the changing nature of family life are crucial in this regard for Giddens.

I want to suggest in this conclusion, in the first instance, that Giddens is substantially correct. That is to say, the experience of reflexivity – while a feature of all social experience, and thus trans-historical – has been consolidated, extended and transformed in our own time of advanced globalization and new information technologies. The "constant examination and reformation of social practices" in a globalizing world is, indeed, a substantially accurate picture of what life is like for contemporary women and men of the so-called advanced, expensive cities of the West (and, given the logics of globalization, also beyond the West too). But whilst largely accurate, there is also more to contemporary social relations. It is not, simply, that advanced globalization brings with it more reflexivity; it also ushers into existence the makeover culture of reinvention – its language and its complexities. If the world of the late twentieth and early twentieth-first centuries has been the Age of Reflexivity, it is my conjecture that we are today – in the 2010s and moving forward towards the 2020s – entering the Age of Reinvention.

This takes us now to consider some final points about the conditions and consequences of reinvention.

On reinvention

Reinvention, I have argued throughout this book, hinges on the emergence of a cultural imperative to transform social practices. This imperative, advanced by business leaders, politicians, personal trainers and therapy gurus, emphasizes that flexible and ceaseless reinvention is the only adequate personal response to life in a globalizing world. It is a paradigm that pervades the mission statement of countless makeover service providers: personal trainers, spas, gyms, weight-loss and detox centres, cosmetic dentists and plastic surgeons all chasing the money that people will spend to realize their reinvention ideal.

Various factors, in conditions of advanced globalization, directly influence why individuals turn to the "reinvention craze"; as well, more people specifically contemplate undergoing the trials and tribulations of makeover culture in order to obtain a career edge. I do not claim that reinvention practices are wholly shaped or determined by recent changes in the global economy. But the new economy has ushered into existence changes of enormous magnitude, and in such a world people are under intense pressure to keep pace with the sheer speed of change. Seemingly secure jobs are wiped out literally overnight. Technology becomes obsolete almost as soon as it is released. Multinational corporations move their operations from country to country in search of the best profit margin. Women and men clamber frenetically to obtain new skills or are discarded on the scrapheap. In this new economy of short-term contracts, endless downsizings, just-in-time deliveries and multiple careers, one reason for new individualist self-reinvention through our pervasive makeover culture is to demonstrate a personal readiness for change, flexibility and adaptability.

The reinvention craze paradigm extends beyond the core of the self to the body, that distracting reminder of mortality in a world where disposability has been elevated over durability, plasticity over permanence. The culture of speed and short-termism promoted by the global electronic economy introduces fundamental anxieties and insecurities that are increasingly resolved by individuals at the level of the body. Bodies today are pumped, pummelled, plucked, suctioned, stitched, shrunk and surgically augmented at an astonishing rate. It is not my argument that the cosmetic redesign of the body arises because of the appearance of completely novel anxieties. Previous ages have been plagued by anxiety too, and certainly insecurities pertaining to employment and career prospects are hardly new (Giddens 1991). But the method of coping with, and reacting to, anxieties stemming from the new paradigm of self-making in our global age is quite different to previous times. In contrast to the factory conditioned certainties and bureaucratic rigidities of yesterday's work-world, in which personal insecurities "locked in" tightly with the organizational settings of economic life, today's new corporatism is a world in which individuals are increasingly left to their own devices as regards their working life and its future prospects. This is a societal change that creates considerable scope for personal opportunities, but it is also one that involves severe stresses and emotional costs. Today's faith in flexibility, plasticity and incessant reinvention throughout the corporate world means that employees are judged less and less on previous achievements, on their records. Rather people are assessed, and ever more so, on their willingness to embrace change, their adaptability for personal makeover. In such circumstances, anxiety becomes free-floating, *detached* from organizational life. Consequently, anxiety rounds back upon the self. In such circumstances, many feel an increased pressure to improve, transform, alter and reinvent themselves. Today's makeover culture arises in this social space, in response to such ambient fears.

Just as flexible capitalism engages in ceaseless organizational restructurings, so now do people – employees, employers, consumers, parents and children. Don DeLillo argues that global capitalism generates transformations at "the speed of light", not only in terms of the sudden movement of factories, the mass migration of workers and the instant shifts of liquid capital, but in "everything from architecture to leisure time to the way people eat and sleep and dream" (1998:786). In thinking about the complex ways in which our emotional lives are altered by the socio-economic changes wrought by globalization, I seek to add to the wealth of transformations mentioned by DeLillo by focusing on people's changing experiences of their identities, emotions, affects and bodies as a result of new individualist social practices. My argument is that global forces, in transforming economic and technological structures, penetrate to the very tissue of our personal and emotional lives.

Most writers agree that globalization involves the dramatic rewriting of national and local boundaries. The overnight shifts of capital investment, the transnational spread of multipurpose production, the privatization of government-owned institutions, the endless remodelling of finance, the rise of new technologies and the unstable energy of 24/7 stock markets: such images of multinational capitalism bring starkly into focus the extent to which today's globe is being remade, and daily. I have been suggesting that such changes seep deeply into daily life, and are affecting greater and greater numbers of people. The values of the new global economy are increasingly being adopted by people to remodel their lives. The emphasis is on living the short-term contract lifestyle (from what one wears to where one lives to how one works), of ceaseless cosmetic transformations and bodily improvements, of instant metamorphosis and multiple identities. This is the field of reinvention society, as it continues to spread across the polished, expensive cities of the West and beyond.

FURTHER READING

Anthony Elliott and Charles Lemert, *The New Individualism: The Emotional Costs of Globalization*, 2nd Edition, London and New York: Routledge, 2009.

Anthony Elliott: *Making The Cut: How Cosmetic Surgery is Transforming Our Lives*, London: Reaktion Books, 2008.

Zygmunt Bauman, *Liquid Life*, Cambridge: Polity, 2005.

Julia Kristeva, *New Maladies of the Soul*, Columbia University Press, 1997.

Anthony Giddens, *Modernity and Self-Identity*, Cambridge: Polity, 1991.

REFERENCES

Amman, J., Carpenter, T., and Neff, G. (eds) (2007) *Surviving The New Economy*. Boulder, CO: Paradigm Publishers.

Andrews, Darrell (2011) "The Key to 21st Century Career Success!" 6 February, http://coachdspeaks.com/reinvention-the-key-to-21st-century-career-success/ (accessed July 2012).

Anthony, Scott D., and Putz, Michael (2009) "To Reinvent Your Company, Reinvent Yourself", 18 May, http://www.forbes.com/2009/05/18/reinvention-entrepreneur-kegan-leadership-clayton-christensen-creative-disruption.html (accessed July 2012).

Ballard, J.G., and Baudrillard, Jean (1998) *The Consumer Society: Myths and Structures*. London: Sage.

Bauman, Zygmunt (2004) *Wasted Lives: Modernity and Its Outcasts*. Cambridge: Polity.

Benckler, Yochai (2006) *The Wealth of Networks: How Social Production Transforms Markets and Freedom*. New Haven, CT: Yale University Press.

Braudy, Leo (1997) *The Frenzy of Renown*. New York: Vintage Books.

Capra, Fritjof (1996) *The Web Of Life: A New Scientific Understanding of Living Systems*. New York: Anchor Books.

Danns, Jennifer Hayashi (2011) *Stripped*. Forest Row, East Sussex: Clairview Books.

DeLillo, Don (1998) *Underworld*. New York: Simon and Schuster.

The Economist (2009) "Reshaping Cisco: The world according to Chambers", 27 August, http://www.economist.com/node/14303574 (accessed July 2012).

Elliott, A. (2007) *Concepts of the Self*. Cambridge: Polity. 2nd Edition.

—— (2008) *Making the Cut: How Cosmetic Surgery is Transforming our Lives*. Chicago: University of Chicago Press.

Elliott, A. and Lemert, C. (2009) *The New Individualism: The Emotional Costs of Globalization*. London and New York: Routledge. 2nd Edition.

Elliott, A. and Urry, John (2010) *Mobile Lives*. London and New York: Routledge.

Foucault, M. (1978) *The History of Sexuality Volume 1: An Introduction*. New York: Vintage Books.

Freeman-Greene, Suzy (2009) "Raunch culture and the growth of the 'designer vagina'", *The Age*, 20 November, http://www.theage.com.au/opinion/society-and-culture/raunch-culture-and-the-growth-of-the-designer-vagina-20091119-iotc.html (accessed July 2012)

Furedi, Frank (2003) *Therapy Culture: Cultivating Vulnerability in an Uncertain Age*. London: Routledge.

Giddens, A. (1990) *The Consequences of Modernity*. Cambridge: Polity.

—— (1991) *Modernity and Self-Identity: Self and Society in the Late Modern Age*. Cambridge: Polity.

—— (2002) *Runaway World: How Globalisation Is Reshaping Our Lives*. London: Profile Books. 2nd Edition.

Granovetter, Mark S. (1983) "The Strength of Weak Ties: A Network Theory Revisited", *Sociological Theory*, Vol. 1, pp. 203–33.

Han, Sam (2011) *Web 2.0*. London and New York: Routledge.

Kasarda, John D. (2008) "The Evolution of Airport Cities and the Aerotropolis", in *Airport Cities: The Evolution*. London: Insight Media.

Kundera, M. (1995) *Slowness*. New York: HarperCollins.

Landsberg, Mitchell (2011) "Leaders of Conservative Judaism press for change as movement's numbers drop", *Los Angeles Times*, 12 April, http://articles.latimes.com/2011/apr/12/local/la-me-conservative-jews-20110412 (accessed July 2012).

Lasch, Christopher (1991) *The Culture of Narcissism: American Life in an Age of Diminishing Expectations*. New York and London: W. W. Norton.

Lofton, Kathryn (2011) *Oprah: The Gospel of an Icon*. Berkeley: University of California Press.

Lupton, Deborah (2012) *Fat*. London: Routledge.

Lury, Celia (2011) *Consumer Culture*. Cambridge: Polity. 2nd Edition.

Mallozzi, Vincent M. (2009) "Answers to life's worries, in three-minute bursts", *The New York Times*, 30 August, http://www.nytimes.com/2009/08/31/nyregion/31therapy.html (accessed July 2012).

McEwan, Ian (1987) *The Child in Time*. New York: Random House.

Milgram, Stanley (1967) "The Small World Problem", *Psychology Today*, Vol. 1, No. 1 (May), pp. 61–67.

Mitchison, Amanda (2012) "How the world fell in love with quick-fix weight loss", http://www.guardian.co.uk/lifeandstyle/2012/feb/24/quick-fix-weight-loss (accessed July 2012).

Moskowitz, Eva S. (2001) *In Therapy We Trust*. Baltimore, MD: Johns Hopkins University Press.

Perrucci, Robert, and Perrucci, Carolyn C. (2007) *The Transformation of Work in the New Economy: Sociological Readings*. Los Angeles, CA: Roxbury Publishing Company.

Poague, Leland (ed.) (1995) *Conversations with Susan Sontag*, Jackson: University Press of Mississippi.

Rieff, Philip (1965) *The Triumph of the Therapeutic: Uses of Faith after Freud*. New York: Harper and Row.

Salkeld, Luke (2011) "Didn't get the job? Blame 'lookism', as discrimination against the ugly 'is the new racism'", *Mail Online*, 5 September, http://www.dailymail.co.uk/news/article-2033782/Didnt-job-Blame-lookism-discrimination-ugly-new-racism.html (accessed 2 July 2012).

Schawbel, Dan (2011) "5 Clever Ways to Get a Job Using Social Media", *Mashable Media*, 19 June, http://mashable.com/2011/06/19/get-job-using-social-media/ (accessed July 2012).

Sennett, Richard (1998) *The Corrosion of Character: The Personal Consequences of Work in the New Capitalism*. New York: W.W. Norton.

Shapiro, Susan (2009) *Speed Shrinking*. New York: St. Martin's Press.

Sontag, Susan (2004) "What have we done?", the *Guardian*, 24 May, G2, p. 3, http://www.commondreams.org/views04/0524–09.htm (accessed July 2012).

Soros, George (1998) *The Crisis of Global Capitalism: Open Society Endangered*. London: Little, Brown.

Turkle, Sherry (1995) *Life On The Screen: Identity in the Age of the Internet*. New York: Simon and Schuster.

Urry, John (2007) *Mobilities*. Cambridge: Polity.

Warhol, Andy (1976) *The Philosophy of Andy Warhol (From A to B and Back Again)*. London: Pan.

Warshaw, Douglas Alden (2011) *Pulling off the ultimate career makeover*, 21 June, http://management.fortune.cnn.com/2011/06/21/pulling-off-the-ultimate-career-makeover/ (accessed July 2012).

White, Mimi (1992) *Tele-advising: Therapeutic Discourse in American Television*. Chapel Hill: University of North Carolina Press.

Wind, Jerry, and West, Jr., Alfred P. (1991) "Reinventing the Corporation", *Chief Executive,* Vol. 71 (October), pp. 72–75.

Wurtzel, Elizabeth (1995) *Prozac Nation*. New York: Riverhead Books.

INDEX